Facts, Fakes and Fellowship

A Mission 119 Guide to John's Epistles

Hutson Smelley

Facts, Fakes, and Fellowship

Copyright © 2025 Hutson Smelley

Unless otherwise indicated, Bible quotations are taken from The King James Bible.

ISBN: 978-0-9861336-7-1

Other Works by the Author

Better with Jesus: A Mission 119 Guide to Hebrews (2015)

Love, Romance and Intimacy: A Mission 119 Guide to the Song of Solomon (2016)

Chasing Jonah: A Mission 119 Guide to Jonah (2018)

Deconstructing Calvinism - Third Edition (2019)

Living Hope: A Mission 119 Guide to First Peter (2019)

Looking Forward, Living Now: A Mission 119 Guide to Zechariah (2020)

Enduring Storms: A Mission 119 Guide to James (2021)

Dedication

This volume of the Mission 119 Series is dedicated to the educators that invested in me, without whom most of my successes and this book would not have happened. They taught in diverse fields including mathematics, literature, history, law, and theology, not only imparting information but a love for learning as a worthy and beneficial enterprise in itself, the curiosity to ask why and the motivation to find the answer. I hope in some small way to have paid it forward.

Table of Contents

Preface to the Mission 119 Series

The psalmist declares, "Thy word is a lamp unto my feet, and a light unto my path." (Psalm 119:105) The Bible is unlike all other books, not only in its grandeur and scope, but because its words are God's Words. The Bible presents to us God's special revelation of Himself, His biased view of history past and future, the reality of who we are, and a picture of all that we can be. Woven within its pages and spilling over is God's redemptive plan for humanity, with Jesus Christ as centerpiece. We do not study the Bible merely to accumulate head knowledge, but with the earnest expectation of knowing God more and drawing near to Him. Each page has something for us, sometimes encouraging us, sometimes reproving us, always revealing God, and every jot and tittle a precious morsel for our souls. Against the backdrop of a world in darkness, it is the light of truth that pierces through all the deceptions and puts reality in clear focus.

Every generation faces challenges, and the present generation is challenged about truth and whether any absolute truths are knowable. Like all the ones before it, this generation needs to hear God's Word taught boldly, with clarity, without apology, in grace and love. And this generation needs to be reminded by those who teach that the Bible was written for everyone. God has spoken with clarity so that all believers who come to the Bible yielded to what God has for them can know its truths as they grow and mature. The aim here is to strike the proper balance between too little detail to elucidate the message and superfluous detail that obscures, so that this volume is accessible and profitable to laypersons and teachers alike who seek to understand the author's original intended meaning and the continuing relevance of that message today. With this in mind, the Mission 119 Series is designed to provide guidance for the exposition of books of the Bible with depth and a commitment to a plain sense interpretation tethered first and foremost to the context and flow of argument of the book under consideration before comparison is made to other books and the perceived systematic theology of the Bible. Of a certainty, the Bible has one author and contains neither error nor contradiction, but each of the 66 books and letters in the Bible must be allowed first to speak for itself as the teacher helps learners see the message of the book in context and its application principles.

A common sentiment today is that people need only "relevant" teaching from the Bible, which suggests portions of the Bible are irrelevant, and too often means they want three steps to raising teens in place of the perfections of God, five steps to a better marriage in place of how a believer matures and walks in the Spirit, how to find blessing and wealth in place of God's demand for holy living, and so forth. May I say that every word God ever spoke was relevant and remains so today. Those who would step forward as teachers of the Word of God only do people a disservice by trying to conform God's Holy Word to the world's bankrupt self-help counterfeits when what is most needful today is the plain teaching of the whole Bible as it is. Believers engaged in the Word and yielding to the Holy Spirit will find the most practical of wisdom and grace enablement for all areas of their lives as they draw near to God in the transformative experience of knowing Him more and more. May I also suggest that while some people will flee teaching that has depth and conviction, far more people in churches today are thirsty for more depth in the teaching. They want to see that the Bible is not clichés and recycled sugar sticks but truly a light from God unto their paths. In this vein, it is my prayer that this volume of the Mission 119 Series will be a useful guide for teachers of the Bible and a special blessing for students of the Word who aspire to know God more.

Chapter 1

Introductory Matters

The epistle we call First John is every bit as relevant today as when it was written in the first century. At a macro level, it is a letter to Christians that is both encouraging and a sober warning against the disastrous consequences of embracing the secular world and its deceptive ideologies. In so many ways, it is the perfect prescription for America's churches who fancy that they can swim in the world's pool without drinking the water. Unfortunately, the letter has been exegetically hijacked in the last hundred years. Our flesh recoils at God's grace and prefers performance metrics that separate genuine from spurious Christians based on subjectively perceived levels of obedience. This man-centered approach to the Bible sowed legalism in fields of grace and reaped a neo-Phariseeism that pats its own back for taking a stand against sin in the church while blind to its own self-righteousness. This theological commitment has been employed to the fullest with First John, even to the point of emending the inspired text to force open an exegetical crack in the door where there was none before. The disheartening irony of this development is that it unwittingly uses First John to sow doubt among believers just like the false teachers (antichrists) in the crosshairs of the epistle sought to do. Fortunately, in recent years, others have championed a workable and contextually driven interpretation that reclaims the power and relevance of the epistle for Christians today, not as a polemic against spurious Christians but an encouragement about the benefits of walking in fellowship with the Father and the Son in the last hour. It is to their voices that this commentary is added.

Authorship and Date

Notwithstanding that First John never identifies its author, "[e]arly Christian tradition ascribes 1 John to the apostle John."[1] As Kruse explains, "Irenaeus (d. a.d. 202), Dionysius of Alexandria (d. ca. a.d. 265), and Tertullian (d. after a.d. 220) all ascribe the authorship of the Fourth Gospel and 1 John unequivocally to John the disciple and apostle of the Lord."[2] He concludes that "early Christian tradition is unanimous in ascribing 1 John to John, the disciple and apostle of the Lord."[3] While First John does not identify its author, it does confirm the author was an eyewitness of Jesus' teaching ministry, and nothing within the epistle excludes John as the author. In addition, if it is granted that the apostle John authored the book we call the Gospel of John, this further supports John's authorship of First

---

[1] Colin G. Kruse, *The Letters of John*, The Pillar New Testament Commentary (Grand Rapids, MI; Leicester, England: W.B. Eerdmans Pub.; Apollos, 2000), 11.

[2] Ibid., 11.

[3] Ibid., 14.

John. Indeed, "[t]he writing [First John] is so closely connected with the Fourth Gospel in vocabulary, style, thought, scope, that these two books cannot but be regarded as works of the same author (see § 8)."[4] As Bruce Barton and Grant Osborne similarly observe: "The similarities between the Gospel of John and these letters identified as 1, 2, and 3 John are so remarkable that it would be difficult to argue that these writings were done by two different people."[5] They further note that "according to the earliest traditions of the church, John wrote all four books from Ephesus."[6]

The question of when the epistle was written is more challenging. Historically, conservative scholars have placed the writing late in the first century. As Marshall explains, "it has long been customary to date the Epistles fairly late in the first century, largely on the basis of a similar dating for the Gospel of John."[7] Barton and Osborne place John's Gospel around A.D. 80-85, and First John around A.D. 85-90.[8] Kruse similarly places the writing of John's Gospel around A.D. 85-90, and on that basis "places the writing of 1 John in the early part of the last decade of the first century."[9] Others are less certain because "[t]here is no direct evidence to shew, when and

[4] Brooke Foss Westcott, ed., *The Epistles of St. John: The Greek Text with Notes and Essays*, 4th ed., Classic Commentaries on the Greek New Testament (London; New York: Macmillan, 1902), xxx.
[5] Bruce B. Barton and Grant R. Osborne, *1, 2 & 3 John*, Life Application Bible Commentary (Wheaton, IL: Tyndale House, 1998), 1.
[6] Ibid.
[7] I. Howard Marshall, *The Epistles of John*, The New International Commentary on the New Testament (Grand Rapids, MI: Wm. B. Eerdmans Publishing Co., 1978), 47.
[8] Bruce B. Barton and Grant R. Osborne, *1, 2 & 3 John*, 3.
[9] Colin G. Kruse, *The Letters of John*, 27–28.

where it was written."[10] J. A. T. Robinson has made the case that none of the New Testament books need to be dated after A.D. 70.[11] Zane Hodges provides a candid appraisal when he writes that "[v]irtually nothing in the epistle indicates a specific date or period for its writing."[12] Nevertheless, he argues that "a good case can be made for dating the Gospel of John sometime prior to A.D. 70," and for that reason it is unnecessary to assign First John to the late first century.[13]

Recognizing that "there is very little concrete evidence one way or the other," Marshall points out that the date we assign for First John "must allow adequate time for the growth of the false teaching reflected in 1 John and the development of the ecclesiastical situation."[14] He cautions against dating the "Epistles too early," opting for "a date between the sixties and nineties of the first century," and further cautions that "it would be rash to attempt greater precision in the lack of more concrete evidence."[15] Given the dearth of evidence, there is no room for dogmatism about the date, and of course, at the end of the day it does not change the meaning of the book. That said, many assume that Gnosticism or pre-gnostic ideas came too late in the first century for First John to have been written before AD 70, but it seems likely that the Gnostic heresies in some form predate AD 70. In fact, the false teachers

---

[10] Brooke Foss Westcott, ed., *The Epistles of St. John*, xxxii.

[11] I. Howard Marshall, *The Epistles of John*, 47–48.

[12] Zane C. Hodges, "1 John," in *The Bible Knowledge Commentary: An Exposition of the Scriptures*, ed. J. F. Walvoord and R. B. Zuck, vol. 2 (Wheaton, IL: Victor Books, 1985), 882.

[13] Ibid.

[14] I. Howard Marshall, *The Epistles of John*, 47–48.

[15] Ibid.

Jude warned about, as Edward Pentecost concludes, may have been Gnostics or pre-Gnostics, and Jude's epistle parallels portions of Second Peter, which itself was likely written around AD 67-68.[16] As with John, there is debate as to when Jude wrote his epistle, but there is no reason it could not have also occurred before AD 70, close in time to the writing of Second Peter. Regardless, it is clear that Gnosticism, not yet in a fully developed form, could have been around before AD 70. Accordingly, a date from the sixties to the nineties is possible.

Audience

In contrast to books like Romans or Ephesians, which were written in the first instance to identified local churches, First John does not identify its intended audience. We may safely assume the epistle was intended to be circulated among several churches. John frequently referred to "we" in his epistle, seemingly to include himself and some of his fellow apostles (or others that witnessed the incarnation), which suggests that he possibly wrote from Jerusalem where we might expect the apostles to be. If that is the case, it would further support the possibility that First John was written before AD 70. In any event, John indicated a state of fellowship with his readers, and frequently referred to them as his beloved friends and little children, suggesting personal knowledge and an ongoing ministry relationship. That being the case, John likely wrote from a church setting to nearby churches. Possibly these local churches were in the

---

[16] Edward C. Pentecost, "Jude," in *The Bible Knowledge Commentary: An Exposition of the Scriptures*, ed. J. F. Walvoord and R. B. Zuck, vol. 2 (Wheaton, IL: Victor Books, 1985), 918.

Roman province of Asia (Turkey) as church tradition suggests.[17] This would find further confirmation in the fact that John wrote the Revelation from Patmos, off the coast of the Roman province of Asia.

Two Camps on the Purpose of First John

Commentators on First John are largely divided into two camps in their understanding of the primary purpose of the epistle. The debate is not academic. How we perceive the primary purpose of the epistle shapes our exegesis throughout. For this reason, this issue deserves careful attention at the outset of this commentary.

In one camp are those that hold that First John is primarily about whether we have a *relationship* with God, i.e., whether or not we are saved and going to heaven.[18] To the extent that this camp sees tests within First John to determine whether someone has a relationship with God through Jesus Christ, this view may be described as the "tests for life" view, using the terminology of commentator Robert Law. In the other camp are those that hold that First John is primarily about whether Christians have *fellowship* with God, which we may think of as "the enjoyment of a relationship" with God.[19] This view is often described as the "tests for fellowship" view. The tests for life view is not well supported by the text nor workable in our daily walk. The tests for fellowship view finds better support in the text, but it is critical that the reader not cabin the entire epistle as either tests for

---

[17] Zane C. Hodges, "1 John," in *The Bible Knowledge Commentary*, 880–881.

[18] David R. Anderson, *Maximum Joy: 1 John—Relationship or Fellowship?* (Grace Theology Press, 2013), 10.

[19] Ibid.

life or tests for fellowship. Any view of the primary purpose of the book as tests misses the larger picture. After addressing the weaknesses of the tests for life view, I will turn to the big picture and how fellowship fits in.

As Gary Derickson explains, "[w]ithin modern-day scholarship two distinct and disparate views have developed concerning the message of 1 John...These are the Tests of Life (Salvation) and Tests of Fellowship (Practice of Life) views."[20] The tests of life view was popularized over 100 years ago by Robert Law's commentary, *The Tests of Life*, in which he argues: "The theme of the whole Epistle, moreover, is Life. Its whole scope is summed up in this: 'These things write I unto you, that ye may know that ye have eternal life' (5¹³)."[21] He explains that "the practical purpose for which it is avowedly written is a purpose of testing" and to "exhibit those characteristics of the Christian life, each of which is an indispensable criterion, and all of which conjointly form the incontestable evidence of its genuineness, is the aim that determines the whole plan of the Epistle and dictates almost every sentence."[22] As Dillow observes: "Advocates of the Reformed doctrine of perseverance understand 1 John to provide several tests by which a professing believer or others can discern whether he is truly born again."[23] By this reasoning, John's exhortations do not concern what his Christian readers *should* do, but establish the "indispensable criterion" of visible works

---

[20] Gary W. Derickson, "What Is the Message of 1 John?," *Bibliotheca Sacra* 150 (1993): 89.

[21] Robert Law, *The Tests of Life*, 2d ed. (Edinburgh: Clark, 1909), 45.

[22] Ibid., 208.

[23] Joseph C. Dillow, *Final Destiny: The Future Reign of the Servant Kings, 4th Edition* (Houston, TX: Grace Theology Press, 2018).

that must be present in any genuine Christian. If even one criterion is absent, the test subject is not a Christian. For instance, if someone claims to be a Christian but does not love a particular brother or sister, he or she is not a genuine Christian. Perhaps in the sober realization that this excludes too many from eternal life, proponents of the tests of life view invariably teach that God grades on a curve. They insist the tests do not require perfect obedience, but a slightly lesser standard. Typically, it is argued that the true believer cannot "practice" sin or some similar phrasing that emends John's words. The tests for life perspective on First John has not only taken root but fully blossomed.

As a preliminary observation, it is difficult to imagine a theological work that more fully emphasized the grace of God than John's Gospel, but if Law and others are correct, John's first epistle replaced "whosoever believeth in him" (John 3:16) with "whosoever" keeps his commandments (1 John 2:3), keeps his word (2:5), walks as he walked (2:6), loves the brethren (2:10), and does not love the world (2:15). Assurance of salvation based on the veracity of God's promises in verses like John 3:16 and dozens of others has been exchanged for assurance of salvation based on self-assessments of our good works. The spotlight has moved from God to man. Absolute certainty rooted in the character of God has been exchanged for human subjectivity. While waging war against a perceived pandemic of spurious believers crouching behind the pews in America's churches, real assurance of salvation has been exchanged for spurious assurance, which is no assurance at all. Still worse, grace that is the nature of who God is (John 1:14) and the basis for our salvation has been exchanged for works.

Despite insistence from the tests for life camp that teaching "saving" faith must be accompanied by works is not the same as salvation by works, it obviously is. Basic logic cannot bend enough to allow mere double-talk to cover the invalidity of arguing that "x" and "not x" are simultaneously true. If we cannot enter heaven without "saving" faith plus the requisite works that must flow from "saving" faith, then heaven's door opens only for those with "saving" works. Proponents of the tests for life view try to cabin the analysis around the spurious believer who lives like the devil, but the analysis should center on the character of God because, in truth, each and every one of us lives like the devil sometimes. As we will see, the nature of God is where John makes his stand in this wonderful epistle. Rather than placing caveats, conditions, and fine print on the grace of God, John goes full throttle on pure undiluted grace.

Defense of the tests of life view usually centers on the alleged purpose statement for the entire epistle. In fact, the epistle has several purpose statements including First John 1:4 ("that your [our] joy may be full"), 2:1 ("that ye sin not"), 2:26 ("concerning them that seduce you"), and 5:13 ("that ye may know that ye have eternal life"). Proponents of the tests for life view take First John 5:13 as the overarching purpose statement for the entire epistle, often likening it to John 20:30-31, which they view as an overarching purpose statement for John's Gospel. They note that both purpose statements are found near the ends of the books. This reasoning is not compelling because while John obviously had an evangelistic intent for writing his Gospel that was expressed in John 20:30-31, it is equally obvious that this purpose did not characterize every jot and tittle in the book. Rather, his purpose statement explicitly focused on certain miraculous signs Jesus performed because they validated his Messianic claims, while many other signs were not included. (John 20:30) John selected specific signs for his evangelistic purpose. Those chapters of John's Gospel not focusing on such signs clearly do not fall under the umbrella of John's purpose statement (e.g., chapters 13-17). This observation does not undermine his purpose statement. Instead it recognizes that John's primary purpose need not have been his only purpose in writing the Fourth Gospel.

A writer may have multiple purposes for writing a letter or book, with different parts of the writing fulfilling different purposes. Given that John's singular purpose statement in his Gospel plainly was not intended to be comprehensive of every passage, the tests for life proponents are serving thin soup when they insist that First John 5:13, solely because it occurs near the end of the epistle, is necessarily comprehensive of John's purpose without accounting for the immediate context of 5:13 and the prior purpose statements. The more natural way to understand the epistle is that the interim purpose statements describe their immediate subject matters. Determining the overarching purpose of the book requires a holistic examination of the text, not isolating a verse or half-verse that fits a favored theological creed. Notably, First John 1:3 indicated the author's desire that his readers enjoy fellowship with "us" and with the Father and the Son. This concept of fellowship recurred in 1:6-7, which undoubtedly presented principles about the fellowship introduced in 1:3. Thereafter, John used various expressions to describe fellowship or intimacy with God in functional terms, e.g., walking in the light (1:7), having the truth or the word in us (1:8, 10), being in him (2:5), dwelling in God (2:6), knowing him (2:13), and loving the brethren (3:14). Mechanistically forcing the purpose statement in First John 5:13 over the entire epistle is misguided and unwarranted.

The tests of life view also does not fit John's audience. We can imagine an apostolic writer providing tests for life for an audience he expected to include non-regenerate persons. We see such "tests" in John 3:16-18. We would also expect in that case a more explicit statement that the author believed he was writing to persons who may not have eternal life. We see that in John 20:30-31. Yet in First John we see exactly the opposite – we see what we would expect from a writer who believed his readers were already children of God if not mature believers. John repeatedly referred to audience as his "little children" in 2:1, 2:12, 2:28, 3:7, 3:18, 4:4, and 5:21, suggesting they were the spiritual fruit of his ministry. Nowhere did John suggest doubt that any lacked eternal life. Indeed, John explicitly confirmed his readers possessed life, telling them their "sins are forgiven" (2:12), they "have known him that is from the beginning" (2:13), they have "overcome the wicked one" (2:13), they "have known the Father" (2:13), and the "word of God abideth in you" (2:14). These are hardly a fitting description of lost people or a mixed group. Having received such assurances from the apostle, what place would tests for life have except to undermine the apostle's assurances? Under such circumstances, and in light of the false teachers that John warned his readers about (more about that later), tests for fellowship is the better fit because fellowship was what they stood to lose if they were deceived.

The tests for life view is also unworkable and self-defeating. Such tests are unworkable because they are vague and subjective. Any test that measures works to determine whether a person has a relationship with God through Christ immediately begs the questions of how much works are needed and who makes the call. We must ask ourselves: Am I qualified to measure whether my own works are sufficient? Might I be biased? In my experience, proponents of the tests for life view always think their works measure up, though some candidly admit that a future failure would establish that their works did not measure up. As I write this, a prominent Reformed pastor recently made headlines for his longtime infidelity, which according to his tests for life view proves he was never a genuine Christian, unless of course God grades on a curve – some infidelity is ok but you cannot "practice" infidelity? The tests for life position renders assurance rationally impossible. No matter how certain I may be that up to this point in time my works were sufficient, I may fail tomorrow in a way that invalidates all previously held assurance. These tests for life fall flat in their purported task. They can only provide assurance to those who in their own subjective estimation meet the standard, which presents the danger that we make ourselves the standard. More than that, these tests only assure those arrogant enough to suppose they will never fail in a way that invalidates their prior assurance, no matter how sincere that may have been. At bottom, tests for life advocates give spurious assurance to guard against spurious Christians.

More problematic than the vague subjectiveness of these supposed tests is that John provided no indication God grades on a curve. Throughout the epistle, John's "tests" were binary. One walks in the light or in the darkness (1:5-7), knows God or not (2:3-4), loves his brother or not (2:10-11), keeps his commands or not (3:24), etc. Few would be so brazen as to suggest that they always walk in the light, always love all the brethren, and always keep Jesus' commands. Yet that is what passing the tests requires every day of our lives. If someone loves their brethren most but not all of the time, or loves all the brethren consistently except one particularly difficult brother or sister, then the tests for life advocate must allow that the test subject is a spurious believer, or argue that "most of the time" is good enough because God grades on a curve. The problem is that John's language leaves no room for a curve. His language is always binary, always all or nothing.

As it turns out, tests for life advocates and many Bible translators have tacitly embraced that God grades on a curve by introducing words like "practice" (e.g., 1 John 1:6, 2:29, 3:4, 7-9 in the NET) to translate ποιέω, a word BDAG defines with primary meanings of to produce or to do. The arbitrariness of this choice is evident in other verses in First John where, even in the NET, the same Greek term is translated "does" (2:17), "do" (3:22), and "obey" (5:2) without the addition of "practice" or "practices." Tests for life proponents have particularly struggled to make sense of First John 3:1-10 and in lieu of recalibrating their theology to the text, have opted to emend the text with the word "practice." Thus John's tests allow genuine believers to sin but not practice sin. A challenging text like First John 3:1-10 must be tackled directly and not by revising the text. John really wrote that Christians do not sin and are not able to sin (3:9) and the expositor is charged with taking the text as it is, not as his theological commitment wishes it to be. With emphatic language, John provided the death knell to the tests for life view, but not the fellowship view. Understanding that in

First John 3:1-10, John addressed how Christians in fellowship manifest to an observing world the new nature or the seed of God within them, the reader does not need God to grade on a curve to preserve the relationship. We can accept John's binary statements and so accept that what the Christian stands to lose – not because he practiced sin but because he sinned – is fellowship with God in that moment.

Next to be observed is that in verses like First John 2:28, John emphasized the coming bema judgment for believers, as he did again in Second John. He included himself among those that would stand before Jesus Christ, either with confidence or shame (2:28). The only eschatological judgment on Christians taught in the Bible is that judgment the apostle Paul referred to as the bema seat judgment. (Romans 14:10-12; 2 Corinthians 5:10) What is in view in this judgment is not the believer's destiny, but the approval by Christ of a life well lived and the provision of rewards. (1 Corinthians 3:10-15) If John's primary purpose in writing First John was to provide tests for life to an audience he believed included lost people, it is baffling that he would include this material at all. This material is fitting, however, to hold together a book exhorting fellowship with God that will result in confidence, and not shame, at the bema.

The challenges for the tests for fellowship view center primarily on the reference to eternal life in the prologue (1:1-2) and the final purpose statement (5:13). This is easily answered by John's express desire to warn his readers about false teachers (2:26) who might sow doubts even among believers. These deceivers or antichrists rejected the incarnation (4:2) and so rejected a central component of the gospel message that the Son of God came and died on a cross. The exigencies of the moment demanded that John address matters that might be undermined by those denying the incarnation of the Son of God who manifested eternal life. For an audience John confirmed had the truth (2:21), his primary concern was false teachers pulling his "little children" away from the truth, but a natural secondary concern would be undermining their assurance of salvation. To remedy that, John provided assurance, but did so based on God's promises and not human works. Some may argue that the tests for fellowship view removes consequences for habitual sin, but John argued exactly the opposite point. For John, loss of fellowship, and a resulting lack of confidence at the bema and in our daily prayer, coupled with an experience of death instead of life, was a tremendous loss to the believer that any rational Christian would strive to avoid.

Truth in John's Writings

The occasion for John's epistle was a conflict between two mutually exclusive views of reality. John referred to one view of reality as "the truth." The truth is a view of reality where the triune God's attributes and works, including His redemptive plan carried out through the incarnation of the Son of God, is the cornerstone. John identified the source of the competing view of reality as "the world" or world system, a comprehensive concept that includes people, possessions, pursuits, philosophies, and even religious doctrine. Whereas the truth is centered on the reality of God, the world system is centered on man and materialism and is under the sway of Satan. (1 John 5:19) The Greek noun translated truth can emphasize the quality of being true as well as the content of the truth.[24] In specific applications, it may refer to "the content of Christianity as the ultimate truth"[25] or "an actual event or state, *reality*."[26] A short excursus into John's development of the concept of truth will be beneficial to our study of First John.

The Bible opens with God, who spoke the material universe into existence. As such, reality begins with the person and works of God. John's Gospel opens by introducing the Word, who through the incarnation declared the reality of God to the world. (John 1:18) From the outset then, we observe that "truth" is an attribute of the Father revealed by the Son. When Moses asked to see God's glory, God responded that he would "make all my goodness pass before thee" but added that "thou canst not see my face: for there shall no man see me, and live." (Exodus 33:18-20) For this reason, Moses was placed "in a clift of the rock" and was covered while God passed by. (Exodus 33:22) At that moment, He proclaimed, "The LORD God, merciful and gracious, longsuffering, and abundant in goodness and truth." (Exodus 34:6) Reflecting on that event, John wrote that Jesus displayed "the glory as of the only begotten of the Father, full of grace and truth." (John 1:14) Indeed, the law came by Moses, but "grace and truth came by Jesus Christ." (John 1:17) This is not to be equated with simply being truthful or speaking something that is true. The grace and truth Jesus revealed showed those who beheld him the reality of the Father in

---

24 William Arndt et al., *A Greek-English Lexicon of the New Testament and Other Early Christian Literature* (Chicago: University of Chicago Press, 2000), 42.

25 Ibid.

26 Ibid.

His being. Indeed, "the basic meaning of 'truth' in John" is "God's reality, which, since God is the Creator, is the only true reality."[27]

Understood this way, John wrote in his Gospel of doing truth (John 3:21), worshiping in truth (John 4:23-24), the Baptist's bearing witness of the truth (John 5:33), and knowing the truth which shall make us free (John 8:32). This truth is more than a particular proposition or general quality of truthfulness. As John recognized, "the light shineth in darkness; and the darkness comprehended it not." (John 1:15) Jesus manifested reality from God's perspective, with His nature and character as the cornerstone, to a world system characterized in the Fourth Gospel and First John as darkness. The world system, John warned, was under the sway of the evil one. (1 John 5:19) This referred to Satan, of whom Jesus taught that "there is no truth in him." (John 8:44) The apostle Paul affirmed that Satan is "the god of this world [who] hath blinded the minds of them which believe not." (2 Corinthians 4:4) Marianne Thompson's comments on darkness are insightful: "'Darkness' is not simply equivalent to sin or wrongdoing. It is the realm that opposes and is hostile to God. This realm is characterized by disobedience and lack of relationship to God. Thus John exhorts Christians— and all people—not to walk in darkness."[28] Accordingly, to do truth or worship in truth is to act and worship in accordance with the true reality declared by Jesus. Thompson explains: "It means living in conformity with

---

[27] Leon Morris, *The Gospel according to John*, The New International Commentary on the New Testament (Grand Rapids, MI: Wm. B. Eerdmans Publishing Co., 1995), 260.
[28] Marianne Meye Thompson, *1-3 John*, The IVP New Testament Commentary Series (Downers Grove, IL: InterVarsity Press, 1992).

truth and light, living in accord with the character of God. Those whose allegiance is truly to God will be shaped by that commitment and by God's own character."[29]

While the character and person of God are foundational to the truth, there is more. Jesus proclaimed: "I am the way, the truth, and the life: no man cometh unto the Father, but by me." (John 14:6) By identifying as the truth, Jesus claims his person, and not merely his words, is the message and ultimate revelation of reality. By relating the truth to the way and the life, which are soteriological, Jesus incorporated God's plan of redemption within the truth. Morris recognizes the same from the prologue of the Fourth Gospel: "We should probably consider here, too, the fact that 'grace and truth came through Jesus Christ' (1:17), for this indicates a close link between truth and the gospel of God's grace."[30] In the same discourse as his self-identification as the truth, Jesus promised to send "the Spirit of truth" that "the world cannot receive because it seeth him not, neither knoweth him." (John 14:17) The "Spirit of truth" will testify of Jesus (John 15:26), who in the incarnation perfectly declared the Father, and the "Spirit of truth...will guide you into all truth." (John 16:13). In his high priestly prayer, Jesus prayed that the Father would sanctify his disciples "through thy truth: thy word is truth." (John 17:17) It is notable that in Paul's bleak description of the actions of humanity apart from Christ beginning in Romans 1, he wrote that they "hold" or suppress "the truth in unrighteousness" (Romans 1:18) and "changed the truth of God into a lie" (Romans 1:25). They reject reality as it is and replace it with a counter-reality

---

[29] Ibid.
[30] Leon Morris, *The Gospel according to John*, 261.

sustained by empty thinking rooted in a darkened heart (Romans 1:21), foolishness (Romans 1:22), and a "reprobate mind" (Romans 1:28). Paul's description characterized what John would call the world and darkness.

Pulling together this data, what is at issue when John wrote of the truth is a right view reality anchored in God as declared by the Son during the incarnation, including the working out of God's redemptive plan through the Son and the Spirit. It is not simply that God sent the Son with a message for humanity, but that the Son of God, during his earthly ministry, was the message. The book of Hebrews opened with that same truth. In times past God spoke through prophets but "hath in these last days spoke unto us by his Son." (Hebrews 1:1-2) As Dan Lioy concludes, "the Evangelist refined this understanding by focusing the notion of truth on the Father's revelation of Himself in His Son. An examination of the data obtained from the Fourth Gospel indicates that the divine-incarnate Messiah is both the epitome and emissary of truth."[31] Along the same lines, Morris rightly concludes that the "truth is not the teaching about God transmitted by Jesus but is God's very reality revealing itself—occurring!—in Jesus."[32] Connecting the dots further, Morris states: "The connection with Jesus is essential to the idea of truth as we see it in this Gospel. It starts from the essential nature of God, it finds its expression in the gospel whereby God saves people, and it issues in lives founded on truth and showing forth truth."[33] A primary purpose of First John is that believers would experience

---

[31] Dan Lioy, "The Biblical Concept of Truth in the Fourth Gospel," *Conspectus Volume 6* (2008): 90.

[32] Leon Morris, *The Gospel according to John*, 260.

[33] Ibid., 262.

this reality and reject the counter-reality directed by Satan, represented by the world system, and promoted by the antichrists or deceivers through their lies. As Lawrence Richards concludes: "John's focus is on the link of truth and reality. A thing is true because it is in harmony with reality as God knows reality. We can know (experience) reality only by choosing to keep Jesus' words, which show us life as God intends His children to live it."[34]

The Purpose of First John

The purpose of First John is more multifaceted than tests for life or fellowship. John directed his epistle to Christians, repeatedly referring to them as his spiritual children (2:1, 12, 14, 18, 28; 3:7, 18; 4:4; 5:21) and expressly affirming their status as believers (2:12). At the same time, John understood that the deceptions of the world system, in relentless opposition to the truth, could snare his readers with disastrous consequences. The deceptions included specific false teachers he referred to as antichrists who rejected the incarnation, which as we have seen is the focal point of God's revelation of truth and reality to the world. The key to his readers avoiding being deceived by the antichrists or lured away by the things of the world, and to experiencing many other benefits as children of God, was continuing in intimate fellowship with God. Because God is holy and morally pure, John set out principles for how people that still sin (we all do) can experience fellowship with a holy God. To attempt to articulate the overall purpose of First John in one sentence: The purpose of First John was to affirm John's

---

[34] Lawrence O. Richards, *The Teacher's Commentary* (Wheaton, IL: Victor Books, 1987), 707.

readers as children of God and overcomers who know the truth and have the Holy Spirit, warn them about the dangers of the world and its religious deceivers (the antichrists), and to explain the principles of and exhort them to live in fellowship with the apostles, the Father and the Son so that they would not be deceived but instead would continue experiencing love, righteousness, truth, confidence, and other benefits available to God's children.

Outline

It has been rightly observed that "[t]his book almost defies being outlined due to its symphonic thematic presentation."[35] Lenski wrote that no divisions of the book are satisfactory because of the "repetitions and reiterations that occur through the letter" such that the "letter has no formal parts such as we commonly use and expect."[36] This has caused many to conclude the book cannot be outlined. The difficulty is not a lack of organization within the epistle, but rather, the interrelatedness of the issues John addressed. It is important, however, to recognize that John did not merely repeat himself. He addressed interrelated and interlocking issues and moved back and forth among them digging deeper and pressing forward with a natural flow and impeccable logic. There have been numerous attempts to demonstrate that the entire epistle is chiastic, but invariably some pieces seem to fit well to a chiastic

---

[35] Grant Osborne, Philip W. Comfort, *Cornerstone Biblical Commentary, Vol 13: John and 1, 2, and 3 John* (Carol Stream, IL: Tyndale House Publishers, 2007), 327.

[36] R. C. H. Lenski, *The Interpretation of the Epistles of St. Peter, St. John and St. Jude* (Minneapolis, MN: Augsburg Publishing House, 1966), 365.

format while others are tenuous at best. Likewise, the instances of particular issues or statements coming to the foreground more than once has led to attempts to find several inclusios that might best explain the structure. The difficulty however is that any larger inclusios of material do not demarcate strictly separated sub-units, but instead the various potential inclusios overlap with one inclusio beginning in the middle of another. I have opted to present a standard outline to emphasize the logical flow of John's writing.

I. PROLOGUE – THE INCARNATION AND FELLOWSHIP INTRODUCED (1:1-4)

 a. The incarnate word of life confirmed (1:1-2)

 b. <u>Primary Purpose Statement</u>: That John's readers experience fellowship with the apostles, the Father and the Son centered on the reality of the incarnation (1:3-4)

II. FELLOWSHIP MUST ACCORD WITH THE TRUTH-REALITY OF GOD'S HOLINESS AND MORAL PURITY (1:5-2:11)

 a. Fellowship principles based on light and darkness (1:5-2:2)

   i. God's holiness and moral purity circumscribe the requisites for fellowship (1:5)

   ii. Fellowship with God is not possible while walking in darkness (1:6)

   iii. The blood of Jesus makes it possible for believers to walk in the light and enjoy fellowship with God (1:7)

     iv. To deny our sin nature is self-deception and contrary to the truth-reality (1:8)

     v. Confessing sins brings forgiveness and purification so that we can continue in fellowship with the holy God (1:9)

     vi. To deny we sin denies God's Word (1:10)

     vii. <u>Interim Purpose Statement</u>: That John's little children would not sin, but if they do, they would know that Jesus Christ is their high priest advocate with the Father and the propitiation for sins (2:1-2)

  b. Fellowship principles based on obedience and love (2:3-11)

     i. Not keeping Jesus' commands means we do not know him, but through obedience we can know we abide in fellowship with him and that God's love is complete in us (2:3-6)

     ii. The old command from the beginning of Jesus' earthly ministry to love one another is also a new command because the darkness is passing away and the true light is shining (2:7-8)

     iii. Not loving the brethren means we are in the darkness, but when we love the brethren, we abide in the light (2:9-11)

III. ASSURANCE TO JOHN'S READERS AS OVERCOMERS (2:12-14)

  a. Their sins were forgiven (2:12)

  b. They know Jesus and have overcome the evil one (2:13)

c. They know the Father and the Son, they are strong, God's Word abides in them and they have overcome the evil one (2:14)

IV. WARNINGS ABOUT LIVING IN THE LAST HOUR (2:15-27)

    a. Warning about the allures of the world system (2:15-17)

        i. Love of the world system is incompatible with God's love in us as a controlling influence (2:15)

        ii. The allures of the world system are from the world not God (2:16)

        iii. The world system and its allures are passing away but the one that does God's will abides forever (2:17)

    b. Warning about the antichrists that deny truth in the last hour (2:18-23)

        i. It is the last hour and many antichrists have come who were with the apostles but not in fellowship with them (2:18-19)

        ii. <u>Interim Purpose Statement:</u> That they know the truth-reality and that no lie originates from the truth-reality (2:20-21)

        iii. The antichrists (deceivers) deny the truth-reality about the Father and the Son (2:22-23)

    c. Exhortation to hold to the truth-reality and abide in the Father and the Son (2:24-27)

    i. If the truth-reality abides in you, you will abide in the Father and the Son (2:24-25)

    ii. <u>Interim Purpose Statement</u>: To warn his readers about the deceivers (2:26)

    iii. His readers have the anointing from God, and so do not need to learn from the deceivers, but to continue abiding in fellowship with God (2:27)

V. THE PRACTICAL OUTWORKING OF LIVING IN FELLOWSHIP WITH GOD (2:28-4:18)

  a. Abiding in God will result in confidence at the bema judgment (2:28)

  b. God's children are made visible by their God-righteousness as they abide in God, and the devil's children are made visible by their lack of God-righteousness (2:29-3:10)

    i. God is righteous and those that manifest His righteousness are His children (2:29)

    ii. We are blessed to be God's children, and our sure hope that purifies us is that when Jesus returns, we will be like him (3:1-3)

    iii. All sin is wickedness (3:4)

    iv. The sinless Jesus died to take away sins (3:5)

    v. Those abiding in fellowship with Jesus don't sin, but the one who sins has not seen or known him (3:5-6)

    vi. The one who does God-righteousness is righteous, but the one who sins is of the devil (3:7-8)

vii. God's children don't sin and can't sin because His seed abides in them (3:9)

viii. God's children and the devil's children are made obvious by whether they exhibit God-righteousness, or fail to do so (3:10)

c. The world is hostile to righteousness (3:11-18)

    i. The command they heard from the beginning is to love one another (3:11)

    ii. Cain did not love his brother, but murdered him because his deeds were evil and his brother's righteous (3:12)

    iii. Do not be surprised if the world hates you for being righteous (3:13)

    iv. Love for the brethren confirms we have passed from death to life, but the one who hates a brother or sister abides in death (3:14-15)

    v. We understand love because Jesus died for us and showed us how we ought to love the brethren in action and truth (3:16-18)

d. Those who show God-love for the brethren experience confidence in prayer (3:19-24)

    i. We know we belong to the truth and experience confidence in prayer because of our God-love for the brethren (3:19)

    ii. Even if we have doubts about our motives, we can have confidence that God knows all (3:20)

    iii. If we don't have doubts, we enjoy confidence in prayer and receive our requests because of our obedience (3:21-22)

iv. God commands that we believe in the name of His Son, Jesus Christ and love one another (3:23)

v. The one who obeys enjoys mutually abiding with God and knows from the Holy Spirit that God abides in him or her (3:24)

e. Discern between the Spirit of Truth and Spirit of Error (4:1-6)

   i. Test the spirits to determine if they are from God (4:1)

   ii. The Spirit that confesses that Jesus has come in the flesh is from God, but the spirit that does not so confess is the spirit of the antichrist (4:2-3)

   iii. John's readers have overcome the deceivers, who are from the world and speak the world's words, and the world listens (4:4-5)

   iv. The apostles are from God, and those that know God hear them and those not from God don't hear them (4:6)

f. Love and truth bring fellowship now and confidence at the bema (4:7-18)

   i. Love is sourced in God and failing to love shows we do not know God (4:7-8)

   ii. God's initiating love for us was manifested by sending His Son to be a propitiation for our sins that we might live (4:9-10)

   iii. God's initiating love compels us to love one another and thereby experience God abiding in us and His love completed in us (4:11-12)

iv. The Spirit of truth assures us of our mutually abiding fellowship with God (4:13)

v. Those who confess that Jesus is the Son of God experience mutually abiding fellowship with God and know His love (4:14-15)

vi. God is love, and abiding leads to His completed love in us and confidence at the bema (4:16-18)

VI. EXPERIENTIAL ASSURANCE AS OVERCOMERS (4:19-5:20)

a. Our faith is the victory (4:19-5:4)

   i. The truth-reality is that one cannot simultaneously love God and not love the brethren (4:19-21)

   ii. Those who believe Jesus is the Christ are God's children and love the Father and the Son (5:1)

   iii. We know we love God's children when we love God and obey His commands (5:2)

   iv. We love God by obeying, but obedience is not burdensome because those born of God conquer the world through faith (5:3-4)

   v. The overcomers are those that believe Jesus is the Son of God (5:5)

b. Our victory is grounded in the incarnation (5:6-13)

   i. Jesus Christ came by the water and the blood and that reality is confirmed by the Spirit, the water and the blood (5:6-8)

    ii. God testifies to the truth-reality about His Son, and those that reject that truth make God a liar (5:9-10)

    iii. God testifies that we have eternal life in His Son, and the one without the Son does not have life (5:11-12)

    iv. If we believe in the name of the Son of God, we know that we have eternal life (5:13)

  c. Overcomers have confidence in prayer (5:14-17)

    i. Overcomers are confident about receiving what is requested in prayer according to God's will (5:14-15)

    ii. Overcomers pray for a brother in a sin not unto death, but understand that prayer for a brother in a sin unto death will not be granted (5:16-17)

  d. Overcomers know the truth-reality (5:18-20)

    i. God's children don't sin and are impervious to the devil (5:18)

    ii. The world is under the influence and control of the devil (5:19)

    iii. God's Son has given us understanding of the truth so that we can know and abide in the Son, who is the true God and eternal life (5:20)

  e. Stay away from idols (5:21)

Chapter 2

The Doorway

1 John 1:1-4

The opening verses of First John are the doorway into everything John had to say to his readers. As in every age, there were deceivers out to mislead people about truth and reality. John might have started his epistle with an explicit warning about the deceivers that occasioned the writing. He might have provided an itemization of their heresies. Instead, John opened with the reality of the incarnation of the Son of God, the same reality the deceivers denied. Perhaps John knew there would always be deceivers repackaging their false teaching but ultimately denying Jesus Christ. The antidote to the deceivers, including those that modern Christians are confronted with, is the truth-reality revealed by God through the incarnation of the Son of God. To be armed with this truth-reality and withstand the world system and its deceivers is not a mere academic endeavor where we commit to certain propositional truths. Rather, it is experiential just as the incarnation was experiential. Walking in fellowship with God on the basis of the reality and benefits of the incarnation was the answer, and so would be John's central exhortation to his readers. This fellowship would bring myriad benefits including overcoming the deceivers.

Outline

I. PROLOGUE – THE INCARNATION AND FELLOWSHIP INTRODUCED (1:1-4)

    a. The incarnate word of life confirmed (1:1-2)

    b. <u>Primary Purpose Statement</u>: That John's readers experience fellowship with the apostles, the Father and the Son centered on the reality of the incarnation (1:3-4)

Scripture and Comments

Like the prologue to John's Gospel, the doorway to his epistle is both striking and controversial. The opening words immediately arrest the attention of the reader and set the entire epistle on an other-worldly footing. When Christians think of the teachings of Jesus, they usually think of what he said. The apostle did not take so narrow a view, and neither should we. The conveyed message John drew attention to was the Word or message of life, and that message was fulsomely conveyed through the incarnation – the Son of God in human flesh. Marshall is correct in his observation that "Jesus himself may be meant as the Word who is the source and substance of eternal life."[37] As the epistle unfolds, we will see that there were deceivers circulating among the Christians who denied the incarnation and the cross, which in turn is a direct attack on life.

---

[37] I. Howard Marshall, *The Epistles of John*, 103.

> 1 **John** 1:1 That which was from the beginning, which we have heard, which we have seen with our eyes, which we have looked upon, and our hands have handled, of the Word of life.

Like his Gospel, John started with a reference to **from the beginning**. In his Gospel, those words referred to the opening chapters of Genesis, but it is not the creation event that John had in mind here. Instead, it was **that which was from the beginning...of the word** or message **of life**. Unquestionably, Jesus said a great deal about eternal **life** during his ministry (e.g., John 3:16, 4:14), but John emphasized the unique way in which he and the other apostles (**we have heard...**) received this special revelation from God. The incarnate Son of God was the message. The **word of life** was revealed to the apostles from the very **beginning** of Jesus' earthly ministry. To the extent that the deceivers built their own theology on the denial of the incarnation, what they taught – no matter how it was dressed up – was contrary to historic fact and therefore contrary to reality.

John stressed his personal experience of the incarnation so that his readers could comprehend a truth that transcends academic knowledge. With the imagery of approaching the incarnate Christ from a distance, John described his sensory experience of the **word of life**. First, the message was **heard**, as if from a distance where only the ear-gate was engaged. But as John moved closer, the **word of life** was **seen with our eyes**. At this point the message entered through the senses of sight and sound, but still John remained at a distance. As he moved yet nearer to Jesus, the **word of life** was **looked upon**. In our English translation this may seem redundant of having

seen with our eyes but it is not. The term **seen** is the Greek ὁράω (oraō) which simply means "to perceive by the eye, *catch sight of, notice.*"[38] But the term **looked upon** is the Greek θεάομαι (theaomai) and means "to have an intent look at something, to take something in with one's eyes, with implication that one is especially impressed, *see, look at, behold.*"[39] In other words, John **heard**, then saw, then intently observed the **word of life** close up. And then in words that expressed a face-to-face encounter, he wrote that **our hands have handled...the word of life**. The message, then, included the verbal teachings of Jesus, but John wanted his readers to understand that the Son of God came in human flesh and was the ultimate revelation of God to humanity.

John wrote to Christians, who surely understood he was describing his and the other apostles' personal encounter with Jesus. Deceivers always have a secret sauce theology that aggressively tramples underfoot all that oppose them, usually claiming the proverbial high ground. John did not call out those he aimed to refute as deceivers until First John 2:26: "I have written these things to you concerning those who are trying to deceive you." Even then, he never itemized their false teachings. Instead, he sought to first affirm the truths his audience already knew and the source of that truth. Any competing doctrines had to be measured against the indisputable reality of the incarnate Son of God that John and the other apostles personally witnessed. In his earthly ministry, Jesus fully and completely expressed the **life** of God and no one else could do that.

---

[38] William Arndt et al., *A Greek-English Lexicon of the New Testament*, 719.
[39] Ibid., 445.

We do well at this point to recall that the New Testament frequently extols the significance of the incarnation. The apostle Paul referred to Jesus as "the image of the invisible God." (Colossians 1:15) The writer of Hebrews referred to Jesus as "the brightness of his glory, and the express image of his person." (Hebrews 1:3) In the Fourth Gospel, John wrote: "In him was life; and the life was the light of men." (John 1:4) Continuing, John wrote of Jesus that "the Word was made flesh, and dwelt among us, (and we beheld his glory, the glory as of the only begotten of the Father,) full of grace and truth." (John 1:14) The incarnation is at the center of New Testament theology because "in these last days" God has "spoken unto us by his Son." (Hebrews 1:2) The message God has for humanity was lived out before them in the person of Jesus Christ, fully God and fully human, and the message was **life**. The incarnation is the bedrock of First John and of Christianity. The deceivers that occasioned John's epistle attacked this foundation, and all those that would follow in their footsteps do the same.

> **1 John 1:2** (For the life was manifested, and we have seen *it*, and bear witness, and shew unto you that eternal life, which was with the Father, and was manifested unto us;)

As John continued bringing his readers through the doorway of his epistle, he wrote that **the life was manifested...which was with the Father, and was manifested unto us**. The word **manifested** is the Greek φανερόω (phaneroō) and means to expose or make visible or known.[40] (compare Mark 4:22, 16:12; John 1:31, 2:11) The context indicates that **life was manifested** with the intent

---

[40] Ibid., 1048.

that **life** become known and understood. There is a whole lot bound up in the simple words that **life** was **manifested**. The word **life** is the Greek ζωή (zōē) and can simply mean "life in the physical sense."[41] But here, John wrote that the **life** was something **we have seen...and bear witness** to, **and shew unto you**. These words carried forward the incarnation encounter of verse 1. No one needs an explanation of human "life in the physical sense." John witnessed much more than that.

What Jesus revealed of **life**, John wanted to **bear witness** to, i.e., confirm by his personal testimony, as well as **shew** to his readers. This latter term (**shew**) means to give an account of. Specifically, John desired to give an account of **that eternal life** to his readers—the very **eternal life** that was **with the Father, and manifested unto us** through the incarnation. And so zōē in this instance is a different kind of **life** than mere physical human life because it is sourced in the self-existent God. The lexicon BDAG says zōē can mean "transcendent life" and that is what John was trying to express. The additional adjective **eternal** is the Greek αἰώνιος (aiōnios) and can mean "pertaining to a period of time without beginning or end, *eternal."*[42] Surely that is true of this **life** because it is the very **life** of the eternal Godhead, but it seems that John also had in mind the quality and experiential nature of this **life** – a quality of **life** inherent in the self-existent Godhead *shaped by the holiness of God.* The way in which the self-existent Godhead lives and experiences **eternal life** without beginning or ending was perfectly revealed by the incarnate Jesus Christ during his earthly ministry. This speaks of a

---

41 Ibid., 430.
42 Ibid., 33.

quality and manner of **life** that Jesus himself said could be enjoyed "more abundantly." (John 10:10)

> **1 John 1:3** That which we have seen and heard declare we unto you, that ye also may have fellowship with us: and truly our fellowship *is* with the Father, and with his Son Jesus Christ.

As John continued, **that which we have seen and heard declare we unto you.** John declared to his readers the eternal life Jesus manifested by his incarnation so that they could enjoy **fellowship with us.** The word **fellowship** is the Greek κοινωνία (koinōnia) and commonly means a "close association involving mutual interests and sharing, *association, communion, fellowship, close relationship.*"[43] But it can also indicate participating or sharing something in common.[44] Kenneth Wuest explains: "Again, our word 'fellowship' (*koinōnian* (κοινωνιαν)), has the primary meaning of 'to have joint-participation with someone else in things possessed in common by both,' and the secondary meaning of 'companionship' or 'comradeship.' This person claims to have things in common with God, common likes and dislikes, a common nature, the divine, which basic things eventuate in a communion of interest and activity which we call fellowship."[45]

With this in mind, we need to identify from context what it is that John wanted to share in common with his readers as the foundation of their **fellowship.** On this point, John

---

[43] Ibid., 552.
[44] Ibid., 553.
[45] Kenneth S. Wuest, *Wuest's Word Studies from the Greek New Testament: For the English Reader*, vol. 13 (Grand Rapids: Eerdmans, 1997), 101.

could hardly have been more explicit. He declared **that which we have seen and heard**, i.e., his experience of the incarnation, so **that ye also may have fellowship with us**. It was the incarnation (from the baptism to the cross as he made explicit in the final chapter of his letter) and its implications, the very doctrine under attack by the deceivers, that should bind John and his readers together in **fellowship** if his readers accepted his apostolic teaching. Accepting the reality of the incarnation of the **Son** of God was about more than just a mutual sharing with the apostles. John added that **truly our fellowship is with the Father, and with his Son Jesus Christ**. John's point was that the **fellowship** or mutual sharing he enjoyed, and that his readers could also experience, was with **the Father** and the **Son**. As I noted in the introduction, what John had to say about **fellowship** was in the larger context of his understanding of reality, grounded in the person and works of God declared by the Son during the incarnation. This verse bridges the incarnation to the concept of **fellowship** that is prominent throughout the epistle. You cannot have the one without the other, no matter what the deceivers in the background of John's epistle, and the deceivers today, might teach.

> **1 John 1:4** And these things write we unto you, that your joy may be full.

When John wrote **these things** he looked back to the immediate context of the prior verses. **These things** referred to the incarnation of the Son with the message of life, which can be mutually enjoyed in the community of believers in fellowship with the Father and the Son. John's purpose was to clearly communicate **these things** so that **your joy may be full**. Some readers will note that most

modern translations say "our" **joy** and not **your joy**. As the
notes to the NET translation indicate, a number of
significant manuscripts read "your" rather than "our," and
the Textus Receptus reads "your." While the NET
translators view "our" to be found in the "somewhat
better witnesses," they concede either may be original.
Either way, both readings make sense and are no doubt
true. John's readers (and by application us) would
experience **joy** as they walked in fellowship with the
Father and the Son. Likewise, John confirmed his own joy
when his spiritual children walked according to the truth.
(compare 2 John 12; 3 John 4)

<u>Closing</u>

A hallmark of Christianity is that it is rooted in historic
fact and cannot survive without it. The Bible is full of
history and even when that includes the supernatural, it is
still presented as genuine history. But the centerpiece of
human history, and of the Bible, is the incarnation. This
was not only the maximal revelation of God to humanity
at any time, but what was accomplished through the
incarnation is the foundation of Christianity. God became
flesh and dwelt among us. The Son of God experienced
being human yet was sinless, pronounced to the world
good news and heavenly truths, for the joy set before him
endured a Roman cross for the sins of the world, and rose
again. Without a risen savior who was God in the flesh
there is no Christianity and no possibility of intimate
fellowship with the living God and Creator of the
universe. The world system denies this reality and its
teachers deny the incarnation of the Son of God. It is
fitting and unsurprising that John staked out the historic

fact of the incarnation at the outset, and on that foundation beckoned his readers to fellowship with the Father and the Son.

Application Points

- MAIN PRINCIPLE: John and the apostles were witnesses to the historic reality of the incarnation of the Son of God and John declared what they witnessed to his readers and by application to us as a matter of first importance.

- The intimacy of fellowship with the Father and the Son is available to Christians.

Discussion Questions

1. Why did John describe his experience of the "Word of life" in terms of the physical senses?

2. In the Fourth Gospel, John referred to Jesus as the Word, but in this epistle referred to "the Word of life." What is the difference (if any) and why might John have chosen to make this slight variation in his description?

3. How important is the incarnation of Jesus Christ to Christianity?

4. What do you think of when you hear the word fellowship in a church context? How might John's usage be similar or different from that?

5. John referenced the idea of joy being made full. What is joy? In what way can our joy be empty, half-full or full?

Chapter 3

The Light and the Darkness
1 John 1:5-2:2

The prologue to First John is only four verses but in that short space it grounds the entire book in the profound reality of the incarnation of the Son of God and the startling idea that humans can enjoy intimate fellowship with the Creator. John wanted his readers to experience this fellowship that bridges the finite and the infinite, the created and the Creator, human experience and ultimate reality. John also desired to warn his readers about the dangers of the world system and its false doctrines, but he knew the key to victory over the world was bound up in the incarnation and fellowship. Instead of beginning with the deceptions he sought to expose, John began at the beginning, with the incarnation and first principles. If his readers continued walking in fellowship with God, they would withstand the challenges ahead that were (and still are) inherent in living in the last hour.

Outline

II. FELLOWSHIP MUST ACCORD WITH THE
TRUTH-REALITY OF GOD'S HOLINESS AND
MORAL PURITY (1:5-2:11)

   a. Fellowship principles based on light and darkness
(1:5-2:2)

      i. God's holiness and moral purity circumscribe
the requisites for fellowship (1:5)

      ii. Fellowship with God is not possible while
walking in darkness (1:6)

      iii. The blood of Jesus makes it possible for
believers to walk in the light and enjoy
fellowship with God (1:7)

      iv. To deny our sin nature is self-deception and
contrary to the truth-reality (1:8)

      v. Confessing sins brings forgiveness and
purification so that we can continue in
fellowship with the holy God (1:9)

      vi. To deny we sin denies God's Word (1:10)

      vii. <u>Interim Purpose Statement</u>: That John's little
children would not sin, but if they do, they
would know that Jesus Christ is their high
priest advocate with the Father and the
propitiation for sins (2:1-2)

Scripture and Comments

The incarnation, and especially the cross and the resurrection,
make fellowship possible, as we will see in the balance of

the first chapter. The challenging theological question John needed to answer was how Christians who still have an unredeemed or sin nature could experience fellowship with a holy God.

> **1 John 1:5** This then is the message which we have heard of him, and declare unto you, that God is light, and in him is no darkness at all.

John wrote in 1:3 that what he saw and heard "declare we unto you, that ye also may have fellowship with us." Building on that, he wrote that **this is the message...we have heard of him, and declare unto you**. Jesus said, **God is light, and in him is no darkness at all**. We are to understand that the theological foundation for experiencing fellowship is a teaching John received from Jesus that we find nowhere *explicitly* stated in the four Gospels. Yet it is entirely consistent with, if not implicit, in them. More than that, it is the foundational truth about the character of God in the Old Testament, and as it applies to worship and enjoying fellowship with God, it is the foundational truth of Leviticus. I mention Leviticus here with intention because it is the centerpiece of the Torah and provided ancient Israel its instruction on the nature of God and fellowship with a holy God under the old (Mosaic) covenant. While we are not under the Law covenant today, the fellowship principles in Leviticus were rooted in the nature and character of God and therefore remain true today. These principles provided the theological background for what John wrote about fellowship for Christians under the New Covenant.

The guiding principle is that God is comprehensively and absolutely holy and therefore separated from everything that is not holy, including sin and impurity. Before digging further in the **light** metaphor, the question is raised of what it means to be holy. According to R.C. Sproul in his excellent book *The Holiness of God*: "When the Bible calls God holy, it means primarily that God is transcendentally separate. He is so far above and beyond us that He seems almost totally foreign to us. To be holy is to be 'other,' to be different in a special way."[46] He elaborates further: "[T]he idea of the holy is never exhausted by the idea of purity. It includes purity but is much more than that. It is purity and transcendence. It is a transcendent purity."[47] In a more extended explanation, Sproul further states:

> God's holiness is more than just separateness. His holiness is also transcendent. The word *transcendence* means literally "to climb across." It is defined as "exceeding usual limits." To transcend is to rise above something, to go above and beyond a certain limit. When we speak of the transcendence of God, we are talking about that sense in which God is above and beyond us. Transcendence describes His supreme and absolute greatness. The word is used to describe God's relationship to the world. He is higher than the world. He has absolute power over the world. The world has no power over Him. Transcendence describes God in His consuming majesty, His exalted loftiness. It points to the infinite distance

---

[46] R. C. Sproul, *The Holiness of God*, 2nd ed. (Carol Stream, IL: Tyndale House Publishers, Inc., 1998), 36.

[47] Ibid., 38.

that separates Him from every creature. He is an infinite cut above everything else.[48]

To see the emphasis on God's holiness in the immediate context we need only read ahead a few verses. John contrasted fellowship with walking in darkness and not doing "the truth." (1 John 1:6) He followed this statement by equating walking in the light with fellowship, which is only possible because "the blood of Jesus Christ his Son cleanseth us from all sin." (1 John 1:7) Then he stated that everyone has sin (1 John 1:8) but that God is faithful to forgive our sins and cleanse us from unrighteousness (1 John 1:9). What the immediate context shows is also well supported by the Old Testament usage of **light** and elsewhere in the New Testament including especially John's Gospel.

In the Old Testament, we see light as a symbol for God that is both revelatory and instructive (e.g., Psalm 27:1, 36:9, 43:3, 56:13, 119:105, 130) but is also used to symbolize God's "holiness; light symbolizes the flawless perfection of God."[49] Thompson explains the use of **light** in the Old Testament:

> We can summarize the references to light in the Old Testament under three main headings. First, light attends and characterizes *God's self-manifestation* (Ex 3:1–6; 13:21–22; Ps 104:4). The psalmist pictures God clothed in garments of light (Ps 104:2; compare 1 Tim 6:16), an appropriate symbol for the One who is pure, righteous and holy. Second, *God's revelation* through the spoken and written

[48] Ibid., 36.
[49] I. Howard Marshall, *The Epistles of John*, 109.

word gives light. That word offers moral guidance and direction for living in accordance with God's will. Often quoted in this connection are verses from the Psalms: "Thy word is a lamp to my feet and a light to my path" (Ps 119:105, 130; 43:3; 56:13; Prov 6:23; Job 24:13; 29:3; Is 2:5; Dan 5:11, 14). Just as light shows people where to walk when it is dark, so God shows the way in which human beings are to walk: "in your light we see light" (Ps 36:9). Third, light symbolizes *God's salvation.* The psalmist celebrates God who is "my light and my salvation" (27:1; 18:28), and light is a favorite image of the prophet Isaiah to depict God's saving activity on behalf of the people of God (9:1; 58:8, 10; 60:1, 19–20).[50]

We see these same ideas in the use of **light** in the New Testament. In John's Gospel, Jesus spoke often of life and **light**. He introduced the readers of his Gospel to the revelatory **light** and the life in his prologue:

> **John 1:4** In him was life; and the life was the light of men. **5** And the light shineth in darkness; and the darkness comprehended it not. **6** There was a man sent from God, whose name *was* John. **7** The same came for a witness, to bear witness of the Light, that all *men* through him might believe. **8** He was not that Light, but *was sent* to bear witness of that Light. **9** *That* was the true Light, which lighteth every man that cometh into the world.

---

[50] Marianne Meye Thompson, *1–3 John.*

Jesus possesses life – the "eternal life" of 1 John 1:2 – and Jesus' life was seen of men, and in that sense the "word of life" projects light. John the Baptizer testified that Jesus was "the Light" and the "true Light," uniquely and perfectly manifesting God to a fallen world in "darkness." As Marshall notes, while we do not find this "teaching of Jesus" (i.e., that **God is light**) "in the Gospels in so many words," we do find this teaching in the incarnation:

> [Jesus] was regarded as a revelation of light (Mt. 4:16; Lk. 2:32; Jn. 1:4–9; 3:19–21). According to John Jesus identified himself as the light of the world (Jn. 8:12; 9:5; cf. 12:35f., 46), and Matthew tells us how he commanded his disciples to take up the same role (Mt. 5:14–16). All this implies that the character of God himself is light, and that Jesus was the incarnation of divine light for men.[51]

Indeed, Jesus in the incarnation provided **light** to everyone, especially at the cross and by his resurrection, and those that reject this **light** do so because they love darkness and their deeds are evil. In John 3:16-21, John used **light** to indicate the revelation of God with an ethical emphasis. Because the **light** metaphor describes the character of the One with life, it is completely free of and separated from darkness and sin. We are not surprised to later read that the Son of God, who manifested the Father to the world, would call himself "the light of the world." (John 8:12, 9:5, 12:46) Those who place their faith in him need no longer walk in darkness because they now have "the light of life." (John 8:12)

---

[51] I. Howard Marshall, *The Epistles of John*, 109.

Expounding on John's use of **light**, F.F. Bruce concludes:

> While life is the central thought in this use of
> "light," however, there is in this Gospel the
> further thought of the spiritual illumination
> which comes when God reveals Himself in
> His Word, and this carries an ethical
> emphasis with it. If, despite the entry of the
> true light into the world, men love darkness
> rather than light, it is because their deeds are
> evil (John 3:19–21). Jesus, in His final
> utterance to the Jewish public during Holy
> Week, urges them to believe in Him and so
> become "sons of light," else the darkness will
> overtake them (John 12:35 f., 46).[52]

Returning to 1:5, Jesus said, **God is light, and in him is no
darkness at all**. Though the **light** metaphor is multifaceted
in the Old and New Testaments, John here primarily
emphasized the ethical sense of the **light** metaphor by
relating and contrasting it to the **darkness**. God's moral
attributes (e.g., holiness, justice, love) are maximal, pure,
and completely undiluted by any immorality in the same
way that the pure and true **light** contains no **darkness**
whatsoever. As Bruce explains: "It is in the ethical sense
that John here affirms that 'God is light, and in him is no
darkness at all. God, that is to say, is the source and
essence of holiness and righteousness, goodness and truth;
in Him there is nothing that is unholy or unrighteous, evil
or false."[53] We may also note here that the **darkness** is not
merely sin. The word **darkness** translates the Greek

---

[52] F. F. Bruce, *The Epistles of John: Introduction, Exposition and Notes*
(Nashville, TN; Bath, England: Kingsley Books, 2018), 40–41.
[53] Ibid., 41.

σκότος (skotos), which can mean literal **darkness** but in this context is used metaphorically for "the state of spiritual or moral darkness."[54]

For John, the **darkness** is everything outside of and contrary to the nature and character of God, i.e., **light**. As we will see in what follows, walking in **darkness** is living out of accord with the truth, that is, out of accord with the declared reality of God's character and works including the incarnation. Marianne Thompson says it well: "'Darkness' is not simply equivalent to sin or wrongdoing. It is the realm that opposes and is hostile to God."[55] Thus to say that **in him is no darkness at all** is to contrast the reality of a holy God with a totally incompatible distortion of that reality represented by the world or world system.

The foundational principle that **God is light** raises an obvious question—indeed, the very question answered in Leviticus prior to Jesus' sacrifice at Calvary. If we still have a sin nature and still sin—points John confirmed in the balance of chapter 1—how can we possibly walk in the **light** where there **is no darkness at all**? How can we possibly enjoy fellowship with a holy **God**? It is to these questions that John turned next.

> 1 **John 1:6** If we say that we have fellowship with him, and walk in darkness, we lie, and do not the truth: 7 But if we walk in the light, as he is in the light, we have fellowship one with another, and the blood of Jesus Christ his Son cleanseth us from all sin.

54 William Arndt et al., *A Greek-English Lexicon of the New Testament*, 932.
55 Marianne Meye Thompson, *1–3 John*.

With the central principle in mind that "God is light and in Him is no darkness at all," John explained what we might call principles of **fellowship**. Recall that **fellowship** or κοινωνία (koinonia) means a sharing of things in common, and therefore **fellowship with him** speaks of a mutual sharing of things in common with the God who is **light**, i.e., who is holy, pure, etc. Peter similarly wrote that we "might be partakers of the divine nature." (2 Peter 1:4) It is probable that the deceivers, whose teachings occasioned the writing of the epistle, made a claim of **fellowship**, and as far as John was concerned, their assertion was absurd.

In the first of what was his pattern of instruction, John provided the negative principle and then the positive principle about **fellowship**. Introduced as a hypothetical, John wrote that the person claiming **fellowship with** God, but walking **in darkness**, is guilty of (1) lying and (2) not doing **the truth**. We need to unpack this a piece at a time. Since God is **light** and there is no **darkness** in Him, it is obvious that one claiming **fellowship with God** cannot simultaneously **walk in darkness**. The word **walk** is the Greek περιπατέω (peripateō), which can mean to literally walk, but in this context means to live. BDAG provides the following definition: "to conduct one's life, *comport oneself, behave, live* as habit of conduct."[56] The **fellowship** claim is a lie because God will not and cannot mutually share in any way with **darkness**, but more can be said.

Recall from the introductory material in the first chapter of this book that the word **truth** is the Greek ἀλήθεια (alētheia) and in John's writings frequently conveys God's reality, the cornerstone of which is God's nature and works

---

[56] William Arndt et al., *A Greek-English Lexicon of the New Testament*, 803.

including His redemptive work through Jesus Christ. The **fellowship** claimed by one living in **darkness** is wholly contrary to this **truth**-reality. It is a professed blending of two opposing spheres of living that, like oil and water, the character of God renders impossible. We need to bear in mind that while John may have had the spurious claims of the deceivers in mind, he addressed his Christian readers because Christians can do this. How we live does not save us or "un-save" us, but it can take us of out of **fellowship**. We can enjoy a mutual sharing with a holy God or live in **darkness** but cannot do both at the same time.

On the other hand, **if we walk in the light, as he is in the light, we have fellowship one with another.** In contrast to the Christian living in **darkness** and not in accordance with **the truth**-reality, the Christian living in **the light** enjoys **fellowship** with God and other believers. For many believers, the word **fellowship** means a potluck and good Christian conversation. Those are great but they are not what this verse is about. The **fellowship** we can enjoy with God and with other believers entails participation in something we share in common. As to God, this includes aspects of His nature (He is light) and His purposes. We should reflect His holiness, goodness, grace, love, etc., care about what He cares about, and prioritize what He prioritizes. As to other believers, this includes our common **fellowship** with the holy God as well as our shared belief in the incarnation and its ramifications.

The question posed earlier now gets answered. Christians in their brokenness can still enjoy **fellowship** with God as they **walk in the light** *because* **the blood of Jesus Christ his Son cleanseth us from all sin.** Here, John introduced a verb (**cleanseth**) he used again in 1:9 where he referenced both forgiveness of sins and being cleansed "from all unrighteousness." John used the Greek verb καθαρίζω (katharizō), which can mean to clean (like bathing) but also "to purify through ritual cleansing, make clean, declare clean."[57] Note that John did not write that the **blood of Jesus** cleansed (past tense) **us** but that it cleans (present tense) us. At this point, many Christians object. Some argue that all true or genuine Christians are necessarily in **fellowship** with God. Others question why Christians need any further forgiveness or cleansing of sins. After all, they reason, Jesus paid for all of our sins – past, present and future – at the cross, and we freely received forgiveness of all sins at the moment of faith in Christ. (e.g., Ephesians 1:7; Colossians 2:13) This leads them to insist that John wrote to non-believers who did not know they were lost and therefore needed works-based "tests" for salvation, forgiveness, and cleansing. Yet these objections are based on human reasoning that attempt to draw inferences from certain passages while ignoring the express principles of the believer's fellowship with a holy God that were central in Leviticus, taught elsewhere in the Old Testament, and that Jesus expressly taught. The importance of this cannot be overstated and so I provide an excursus below before returning to the exegesis of First John. The reader already familiar with the purification and reparation offerings in Leviticus may choose to skip the excursus.

Excursus on Fellowship

The apostle Paul argued in Romans 3-4 that justification – God declaring someone righteous – has always been by faith. It is not the case, as is so often misunderstood, that

---

[57] Ibid., 488.

Old Testament saints were "saved by works" but New Testament saints were "saved by faith." Rather, Paul used Abraham as the prototypical example of justification by faith in the Old Testament, quoting Genesis 15:6 to prove his assertion. But if the Old Testament saints were justified by faith, and not by works, then why were the people of Israel required to provide sin offerings to God in order to enjoy continued fellowship with Him? If those who object to First John being addressed to believers are correct because, as they reason, believers need no further forgiveness or cleansing from sin, then the same argument must apply to the Old Testament saints and the book of Leviticus. Abraham and all the others were justified by faith alone and, as the argument goes, needed no further forgiveness or cleansing for sins. But then (generations after Abraham) there is the book of Leviticus standing in defiance of the "believers don't need forgiveness" argument. It is unfortunate that many Christians give little or no attention to Leviticus, which was such a critical part of the "Bible" that our New Testament writers like John knew well.

While we are obviously not under the Law as a binding covenant and the system of animal sacrifices was done away with at the cross, there are timeless principles in Leviticus about the holiness of God and fellowship. In his excellent commentary on First John, Dave Anderson writes:

> God had set up a system to help maintain fellowship between Himself and Israel. This system had nothing to do with His relationship with Israel—that was established, permanent, and eternal (Romans 9-11). But if she wanted to stay in fellowship with Yahweh, Israel had to take advantage of

the system God established for her to be cleansed of her sins. That system was the sacrificial system of the Mosaic Law. It was given for fellowship, not relationship.[58]

Although the sacrificial system is referenced in several Old Testament books, this was a primary subject of the book of Leviticus. The Torah was written in a chiastic pattern with Leviticus at the focal point or center of the chiasm because the book addressed how Israel could maintain fellowship with a holy God. It is critical to understand that all the sacrifices provided for in Leviticus were for believers, some to be done while in fellowship and others for the restoration of fellowship, as Allen Ross explains:

> It is, of course, in Leviticus that we have the detailed legislation for the types of sacrifices that Israel was going to make. These sacrifices may be divided into two groups: those with a sweet aroma and those without. The sweet-aroma offerings were made *in* communion and *in celebration of* communion: burnt offering (Lev. 1), meal offering (Lev. 2), and peace offering (Lev. 3). The non-sweet-aroma sacrifices are made *for* communion: purification offering (Lev. 4) and reparation offering (Lev. 5).[59]

The Levitical sacrifices were not about justification, but fellowship and sanctification. They were the means for God's people – not lost people – to enter His presence and enjoy fellowship. Even though they were justified by

---

[58] David R. Anderson, *Maximum Joy*, 46.
[59] Allen P. Ross, *Holiness to the Lord: A Guide to the Exposition of the Book of Leviticus* (Grand Rapids, MI: Baker Academic, 2002), 79.

faith, continued fellowship required sacrifices for sins and defilement. Allen Ross summarizes this central doctrine:

> God, by his grace, made provision for cleansing sin and its effects so that people might safely enter his presence. This provision was absolutely necessary given the circumstances of life in this world. Sinful acts and defiled conditions of any kind must be dealt with if communion with God is maintained. Even true worshipers, people who are steadfast in their devotion to the LORD and who seek to live in obedience to his laws, find that they need God's gracious provision of cleansing if they are to continue in fellowship with him. They may fall into sin without realizing it, or they may be overtaken in a fault, or they may sin unwittingly; but even these should not be treated lightly. In line with this, the law in ancient Israel clearly revealed that sins of any kind angered God, deprived him of his due, defiled his sanctuary, and thus put a barrier between the guilty and God (Wenham, 89).[60]

The doctrine of Leviticus exactly parallels what we see in First John. God is light and in Him is no darkness at all – no sin, no impurity, no defilement, etc. In the Old Testament, the sanctuary and later the Temple was where God's presence was manifested and His people could worship and commune with Him. If a person had any contamination or impurity of any sort, that also defiled

---

[60] Ibid., 123.

the place of worship and it had to be cleansed before they could enjoy fellowship again. Again, Ross explains:

> But it was not just sin that defiled the LORD's sanctuary and endangered the guilty; the effects of sin were just as serious. Living in this sinful world, one has to deal with contamination, corruption, diseases, and death. And under the Levitical system in Israel these things also rendered a person unclean and defiled the holy place. Leviticus taught that the holy God could not abide with any uncleanness or in a defiled sanctuary. Cleansing was thus required before people with impurities could enter his presence.[61]

The sin offerings or purification offerings of Leviticus 4, and the reparation offerings of Leviticus 5, were provided under various circumstances "to make atonement for sins and defilements so that union with God could be restored. In the case of sinful acts, this involved confession and forgiveness as well."[62] In our English translations we typically read "sin offering" in Leviticus 4, but it is important that we understand that the offering there was not limited to sin. While almost all translations utilize the phrase *sin offering* "following a rather literal and traditional understanding of the word...this sacrifice also dealt with the consequences of sin, the defilements of life that did not require forgiveness."[63] Wenham cautions against the translation "sin offering" because it "obscures

---

[61] Ibid., 123–124.
[62] Ibid., 80.
[63] Ibid., 124.

the precise function of this sacrifice. It most certainly has to do with sin, and deals with its consequences. But it was not the one and only atoning sacrifice, as commentators tend to suggest."[64] This specialized sacrifice differed from the burnt offering and was offered less frequently because the "purpose was purification."[65]

The key issue – and this cannot be overstated – was that the sanctuary itself would be defiled by the believer with the impurity, and that had to be dealt with to restore fellowship. In his commentary on Leviticus, Sklar provides a practical explanation for the need for purification offerings:

> But to the Israelites, sin's defiling effects made an impact not only on the sinner, but also on those associated with the sinner. In this way, sin was like dishonour. For example, when children do wrong, they bring dishonour on themselves, as well as on their family, especially their parents. In a similar way, Israelites who committed certain wrongs brought a defiling dishonour on themselves, their nation (their covenant family) and especially on their covenant Lord. This dishonour clung to the Lord's 'home', the tent of meeting (16:16, 19), just as the dishonour of a child's wrong can cling to the parent's home. It was like an unholy dust that arose from their act and settled on the

[64] Gordon J. Wenham, *The Book of Leviticus*, The New International Commentary on the Old Testament (Grand Rapids, MI: Wm. B. Eerdmans Publishing Co., 1979), 88.
[65] Allen P. Ross, *Holiness to the Lord*, 124.

Lord's sanctuary. How was it to be removed? This section provides the answer: by the purification offering's cleansing blood.[66]

Wenham similarly explains how personal sin creates the need for purification of the sanctuary:

> Purification is the main element in the purification sacrifice. Sin not only angers God and deprives him of his due, it also makes his sanctuary unclean. A holy God cannot dwell amid uncleanness. The purification offering purifies the place of worship, so that God may be present among his people. This interpretation of the term seems to be compatible with its root meaning, and to explain the rituals of blood sprinkling peculiar to it.[67]

Accordingly, the focus of the ritual associated with the purification offerings was purifying various aspects of the sanctuary. David Baker succinctly describes the problem:

> Placing the blood on the altar rather than on the worshiper indicated that the altar (representing the entire Tabernacle because it was the only instrument to which the people had direct access) had been contaminated by an undesirable action or event and needed to be cleansed or purified (Heb 9:23). After the sanctuary had been

---

[66] Jay Sklar, *Leviticus: An Introduction and Commentary*, ed. David G. Firth, vol. 3, Tyndale Old Testament Commentaries (Nottingham, England: Inter-Varsity Press, 2013), 108.

[67] Gordon J. Wenham, *The Book of Leviticus*, 89.

restored through the actions of the priest
and the offerer, then God's action was to
forgive (4:26, 31; Num 15:25).[68]

The mental obstacle for modern believers is that, not
having ever experienced the ritual sacrifices of Leviticus,
we can easily fail to take sin as seriously as we should. The
ancient worshiper who wanted to maintain fellowship
could not help seeing the implications of sin because the
ritual placed those implications front and center. It is not
just the wrong but the consequences of the wrong. Ross
explains that sins required forgiveness because sins defiled
the sanctuary. Indeed, "[t]his is why throughout Lev. 4
the blood of the sacrifice is applied to various sancta in
the sanctuary, but not to the sinner."[69] Our challenge as
modern believers on this side of the cross is to isolate the
fellowship principles and determine how they have
application today.

It is also important to observe that it is not just the work
of the priest that was involved in the purification
offerings to restore fellowship. The believer was
individually involved because the individual needed
forgiveness in order to enjoy restored fellowship, and that
required actions that implicitly or explicitly confessed sin:

> The purpose of the sin offering was to give a
> specific for the penitent sinner who was
> convicted of sin and wished for full
> restoration of fellowship with God. It was

---

[68] David W. Baker, "Leviticus," in *Cornerstone Biblical Commentary: Leviticus, Numbers, Deuteronomy*, ed. Philip W. Comfort, vol. 2 (Carol Stream, IL: Tyndale House Publishers, 1996), 36.

[69] Allen P. Ross, *Holiness to the Lord*, 124–125.

both a confession of his sin and an assurance of pardon. There were representative sin offerings prescribed for leaders of the people as well as offerings for the individual. A type of sin offering was available for the poorest sinner in the land (5:7, 11).[70]

Similarly, Baker writes of the individual's participation through confession:

> The blood of the sin offering brought purification to the sanctuary, which was affected by the sins of the people (Heb 9:23). The offering needed to be preceded by repentance and confession. (Elsewhere confession was tied to laying hands on the offering; 16:21.) Without confession, there would have been no forgiveness; a mere dead ritual would not have worked.[71]

The requirement of confession through certain actions ensured that the process could not devolve into empty rote rituals. Indeed, "it was understood that the one making the offering did so with a heartfelt conviction that he was guilty of sin before God."[72]

With this background in mind, I want to suggest how the Old Testament principles associated with the ritual purification offerings to restore fellowship carry forward

---

[70] R. Laird Harris, "Leviticus," in *The Expositor's Bible Commentary: Genesis, Exodus, Leviticus, Numbers*, ed. Frank E. Gaebelein, vol. 2 (Grand Rapids, MI: Zondervan Publishing House, 1990), 547.

[71] David W. Baker, "Leviticus," in *Cornerstone Biblical Commentary*, 39.

[72] Mark F. Rooker, *Leviticus*, vol. 3A, The New American Commentary (Nashville: Broadman & Holman Publishers, 2000), 121–122.

to New Covenant believers. We know that the animal sacrifices never took away sins. (Hebrews 10:4) We also know that the old covenant with its animal sacrifices has been done away with based on the Jesus' death on the cross. (Hebrews 8:6-13; 10:5-18) Not only that, we know that the Old Testament sanctuary and temple were only pictures or sketches of the true tabernacle in heaven. (Hebrews 8:1-5) Just as the earthly examples required the sprinkling of blood (Hebrews 9:19-22), so also the heavenly tabernacle did, but it required the blood of Jesus (Hebrews 9:23-28). Moreover, we know the old priesthood was done away with. We have a new high priest after the order of Melchizedek (Hebrews 6:20) and Christians are a royal priesthood under the New Covenant (1 Peter 2:9). But with all this in mind, what of the purification offerings and fellowship?

The Old Testament purification offerings addressed defilement of the person and the earthly temple, but the heavenly tabernacle is not subject to defilement. However, New Covenant believers still sin and defile themselves and that is where the purification offering (Jesus) comes in. The body of the New Covenant believer is a temple of the Holy Spirit, and so our personal sins do defile a temple that must be cleansed as a requisite for fellowship. (1 Corinthians 6:19) As Mark Rooker writes: "Just as the sin offering purified the temple, the special place of God's presence in the Old Testament, so the New Testament believer, who has the Holy Spirit residing within, needs purification to maintain fellowship with God (1 Cor 6:19–20)."[73] Ross rightly observes that "moral imperfections and impurities—that is, the sinful activities

---

[73] Ibid., 121.

that rendered a person unclean in the Old Testament—
are still sinful in the new covenant and still require
repentance and confession and forgiveness in order to
comply with God's standard of holiness."[74] I concur with
Ross when he states that "[i]t is folly—it is dishonest—to
argue that because the purification regulations of Old
Testament Israel were fulfilled by the death of Christ, the
sins listed in Leviticus are no longer sins."[75] Stealing,
bearing false witness, and coveting are still sins for which
we need purification. What has changed is that it is only
the worshiper, and not the place of worship, that must be
purified under the New Covenant. Holiness remains "the
basic requirement for maintaining the LORD's Presence in
the life of the New Covenant priest."[76]

Being "saved" does not automatically place us in
fellowship with God any more than it did for those Old
Testament believers. It is true that at the moment of faith
in Christ we are baptized into Jesus Christ and therefore
identified with his death, burial and resurrection.
(Romans 6:3-8) We receive a host of spiritual blessings as
a consequence of our justification including forgiveness of
sins. (e.g., Ephesians 1-2) But these truths associated with
being in union with Christ through faith, what many call
positional truths, secure our eternal destiny as children of
God; they are obviously not the all-in-all for the Christian
walk God wants for us. We know that because the apostle
Paul spilled a great deal of ink addressing how the only
way Christians can manifest the righteousness of God in
their lives is by walking in the Spirit. (Romans 8; Galatians 5)

---

[74] Allen P. Ross, *Holiness to the Lord*, 246–247.

[75] Ibid., 246–247.

[76] Jeffrey Enoch. Feinberg Ph.D. and Kim Alan Moudy, *Walk Leviticus!:
And He Called* (Baltimore, MD: Messianic Jewish Publishers, 2001), 20.

Indeed, to do that is to experience life and peace, but to have a mind set on the things of the flesh is to experience death. (Romans 8:5-6) Paul even warned believers that the wages of sin is death, a statement we find in the middle of his discourse on sanctification that is often misunderstood as a justification truth. (Romans 6:23) But how can believers possibly experience death if their sins are forgiven by virtue of being in Christ?

The answer is that there are two kinds of forgiveness, the first being what many would call positional forgiveness that establishes the relationship on the basis of faith alone, and the second being fellowship forgiveness that provides the means for enjoying fellowship in our daily walk with our Holy God. As I have already shown, that was how it worked in the Old Testament with its purification offerings, and unsurprisingly, that is how it works now. Paul's references to life and death in Romans 5-8 correspond to John's usage of light and darkness. Because of sin, Christians do not always walk in the Spirit and do not always experience life and fellowship. A central purpose of John's epistle was to address how fellowship is restored under the New Covenant.

Before returning to our text in First John, we do well to note the careful division of John's Gospel. Some read the purpose statement in John 20:31 to mean that everything he wrote was for evangelism, but that is obviously not the case. The first twelve chapters are primarily evangelistic and focus on various signs to convince people to place faith in Jesus. As Anderson observes: "In fact, John's signature phrase for a new believer is the Greek construction *pisteuō* eis (believe in). This phrase is found nowhere in Greek literature outside the New Testament, and of the thirty-four uses in John, thirty of them occur in the first twelve chapters."[77] But John 13 was a critical turning point where the focus was no longer evangelism but instead was intimate discipleship.

After Judas' exit during the last supper, Jesus provided his final teachings to the eleven before going to the cross. At that point, the eleven were his "friends," a term indicative of close fellowship, and he taught them "all things that I have heard of my Father." (John 15:14-15) Before providing these new and final teachings and calling them friends, Jesus washed their feet. This act demonstrated humility, but more than that, it provided a critical lesson that cleansing precedes fellowship – the lesson of the purification offerings in Leviticus. Addressing the foot washing of John 13, Dave Anderson summarizes:

> Unbelievers had to come into the temple/tabernacle through the blood, but believers could only go into the Holy Place through the laver of cleansing. The truth Jesus wished to share in the Upper Room was for the ears of believers only. But even these believers needed to be cleansed of their daily sins in order to be in fellowship with the Lord. If they were not in fellowship with Him, they would not be able to comprehend the truth He wished to share.[78]

As we read John 13, we find that Peter initially would not permit Jesus to wash his feet, but then Jesus told him: "If I wash thee not, thou hast no part with me." (John 13:8) Not understanding Jesus' point, Peter responded: "Lord,

---

[77] David R. Anderson, *Maximum Joy*, 16–17.
[78] Ibid., 17.

not my feet only, but also *my* hands and *my* head." (John 13:9) To clear the confusion, Jesus explained: "He that is washed needeth not save to wash *his* feet, but is clean every whit: and ye are clean, but not all." (John 13:10) Jesus clarified that all but one (i.e., Judas) were already "clean." The word translated "clean" in John 13 is the Greek adjective καθαρός (katheros), which in this context means pertaining "to being cultically/ceremonially pure, *ritually pure.*"[79] This is the adjective form of the verb used in First John 1 for cleansing. Jesus excluded Judas from fellowship because he was not clean. The others, metaphorically, only needed their feet washed because they had already bathed. The specific sin that necessitated the feet washing was likely the disciples' pride as they disputed who should have the prominent position in the kingdom, a matter not explicitly stated in John's Gospel but addressed in the other gospels. In addition to the sin was the taint or impurity that resulted.

The feet washing illustrated how the concept of the purification offerings for fellowship in Leviticus apply today. Jesus' work on the cross provides the cleansing that purifies and makes fellowship possible. Again, Anderson captures the point succinctly: "On the relationship level the believer is seen as completely clean (all sins cleansed once and for all time—past, present, and yet future sins); but on the fellowship (intimacy) level the believer needs daily foot washing (daily cleansing from sins in his walk on earth)."[80] With this background, we can turn back to our primary text.

---

[79] William Arndt et al., *A Greek-English Lexicon of the New Testament*, 489.
[80] David R. Anderson, *Maximum Joy*, 17.

Back to First John

Christians still have a sin nature or what Paul called the flesh, and so we still sin. In the Old Testament, a purification offering was required for sin so that a believer could experience fellowship forgiveness and enjoy restored fellowship. But on this side of the cross, we only need the continuing and infinite efficacy of the blood of Jesus Christ. We only need an occasional foot washing to use the metaphor of John 13. John explained that the blood of Christ provides a continual cleansing so that we can **walk in the light** and enjoy **fellowship** with a holy God. Yes, we will still sin, but **fellowship** can be maintained with our Holy God because Jesus provided the purification offering – his **blood...cleanseth us from all sin**. Does this mean we can sin with impunity and remain in **the light**? Of course not, and perhaps that is why John presented the negative example first. If we choose to **walk in darkness** we cannot enjoy **fellowship**. At the same time, John's point is that the Christian walking **in the light** is not permanently thrusted out of **fellowship** into the **darkness** at the moment of sin. The next two verses tie up his point.

> **1 John 1:8** If we say that we have no sin, we deceive ourselves, and the truth is not in us. **9** If we confess our sins, he is faithful and just to forgive us *our* sins, and to cleanse us from all unrighteousness. **10** If we say that we have not sinned, we make him a liar, and his word is not in us.

John presented two negatives to clarify two crucial points about the Christian and **sin**. First, the Christian that claims to **have no sin** (**sin** is singular here) is self-deceived and **the truth is not in** that brother or sister. This example is not about a specific **sin** like adultery, but rather is about our innate propensity to **sin**, i.e., what we might call our **sin** nature. John wrote that the Christian denying his or her sinful nature does not have **the truth** in him or her as their guiding principle. To deny this aspect of humanity is to deny reality, but secular thinking in John's day and today does exactly that. The world insists people are fundamentally good and with the right opportunities and education will be righteous by the current culture's way of thinking about righteousness. Yet the Bible (see e.g., Romans 1) paints a bleak picture of humanity apart from Christ. Unquestionably, Jesus and the apostles taught about our having a sin nature or flesh. On the flip side of the coin, if a Christian denies that he or she has **sinned**, meaning that they have not engaged in sinful conduct, then they make **him a liar**. Here, as is frequently the case, John was not clear with his pronouns because he viewed the Son as perfectly manifesting the Father. The point is that God's **word is not in us** as the guiding principle if we deny our sinfulness because the Bible teaches both that we have a sin nature and personally commit sins.

On the other hand, if **we** acknowledge or **confess our sins, he is faithful and just to forgive us our sins**. It is imperative before diving further into our exegesis that we keep the context in mind, which concerns a Christian living in fellowship with God by walking in the light, not how a lost person becomes a Christian. As I noted earlier, John explicitly confirmed his readers to be Christians. It is careless and misleading to hijack First John 1:9 for evangelism and tell people they have to "confess" all their sins to become a Christian, a task none can do.

The question before us is how Christians, who still sin, can nevertheless walk in the light where there is no darkness at all. Verse 9 answers that question, and based on the earlier notes on the purification offerings in Leviticus and Jesus' application in John 13, the answer is what we would expect. Under the Old Covenant, the ritual surrounding the purification offerings to restore fellowship required confession and provided both forgiveness and cleansing. Under the New Covenant, "the blood of Jesus Christ his Son cleanseth us from all sin." (1 John 1:7) But confession is still required. The verb **confess** is the Greek ὁμολογέω (homologeō) and can mean "to share a common view or be of common mind about a matter" or to admit the truth of something.[81] Just as the Old Testament sinner conceded his or her sin in bringing the offering and participating in the ritual, we also must come in agreement with God about the sins we are aware of.

The word **forgive** is the Greek ἀφίημι (aphiēmi) and means "to release from legal or moral obligation or consequence, *cancel, remit, pardon.*"[82] As Anderson observes, this word is "never used in the Gospel of John when speaking of the relationship between man and God."[83] We so often use the term "forgiveness" or the phrase "forgiveness of sins" in our church lingo about getting "saved" that we may carelessly assume that John would use the same language for evangelism, but we'd be wrong. Anderson points out the glaring omission in John's Gospel: "If the Gospel of John was written to establish an eternal relationship between God and those who believe in His Son (John 20:31), it seems strange that John would not use this word in the sense of God forgiving man in

---

[81] William Arndt et al., *A Greek-English Lexicon of the New Testament*, 708.
[82] Ibid., 156.
[83] David R. Anderson, *Maximum Joy*, 54.

twenty-one chapters ... unless, of course, John reserves that word in his own thinking for fellowship instead of relationship."[84]

Putting all of this together, John wrote that if a believer comes into agreement with God that specific thoughts, words, or actions were sinful, on the basis of Jesus' sacrifice, God **is faithful and just to forgive** the **sins, and to cleanse** the believer **from all unrighteousness**. God is **faithful** in that we can depend on the promise provided in this verse. The word **just** translates the Greek adjective δίκαιος (dikaios) and is often translated as "righteous" (e.g., Romans 3:10, 5:7), and in fact is usually so translated in First John (2:1, 29; 3:7, 12). The reason God is **just** or righteous in His forgiveness is because of the continuing vitality of the blood of Jesus Christ. (1 John 1:7) While Jesus' finished work on the cross paid it all when it comes to the penalty of sin, that does not mean there are no temporal consequences in this lifetime when we sin. It would be surprising if we could maintain fellowship with a holy God regardless of our actions, and certainly that would fly in the face of the material covered earlier from Leviticus. When a Christian sins, the Christian's legal status as a child of God is never in jeopardy, but the Christian's fellowship can be lost by a choice to sin and then not **confess**. When we **confess** the **sins**, we are completely cleansed, not only of the sin we confessed but of **all unrighteousness** (i.e., taint, uncleanness, impurity), and so are restored to the privilege of walking in the light. I hasten to add that this is not a generic request to forgive unspecified **sins**, but a prayer identifying the specific sin or **sins** the Christian is aware of.

---

[84] Ibid., 54.

1 **John 2:1** My little children, these things
write I unto you, that ye sin not. And if any
man sin, we have an advocate with the
Father, Jesus Christ the righteous: 2 And he
is the propitiation for our sins: and not for
ours only, but also for *the sins of* the whole
world.

John addressed his readers as his **little children**, an
expression he heard years earlier from Jesus (John 13:33)
and repeatedly used in his epistle. John saw his readers as
his spiritual **children** because of his relationship to them
in the faith. This not only confirms John's view of his
readers as fellow Christians, but also that he had a
personal role in either evangelizing them or ministering to
them, or both. Having just addressed the issue of **sin** and
forgiveness in relation to fellowship with God, John had
more to say. First, nothing John wrote about the reality
that Christians **sin** was intended to promote or license **sin**.
Perhaps someone might conclude they can decide to
intentionally sin when it pleased them with a plan to
confess after the fact. Yet that kind of thinking reflects
being out of fellowship already and is contrary to John's
teaching. John wrote **these things** so **that ye sin not**. He
intended by addressing the matter of confession to
emphasize the seriousness of **sin**, not to encourage or
excuse it. John's purpose was to promote a Christian life
in fellowship with the living God who is light and in
whom is no darkness. (1 John 1:5) At the same time, John
recognized the reality of **sin** and addressed how Christians
should deal with known sins through confession.

Next, John added more theological foundation for the
concept of confessing known sins as part of our walk in

the light: **if any man sin, we have an advocate with the Father, Jesus Christ the righteous.** The word **advocate** is the Greek παράκλητος (parakletos) and is translated in other places as "comforter" (John 14:16, 26; 15:26, 16:7). The Latin writers used *advocatus* and hence the KJV use of **advocate.** We probably should not interpret the term as "defense attorney" although that preaches well. As BDAG explains: "In the few places where the word is found in pre-Christian and extra-Christian literature as well it has for the most part a more general sense: one who appears in another's behalf, *mediator, intercessor, helper.*"[85] I included in the earlier notes an excursus on the purification offerings in Leviticus, and the notes on First John 1:7-9 explained how that applies to New Covenant believers. Jesus' role as our **advocate** should be understood to relate to what John already said about confession, fellowship forgiveness, and the cleansing blood.

Jesus is our high priest after the order of Melchizedek. (Hebrews 2:17, 3:1, 4:14-15, 8:1) In this continuing role, Jesus is our **advocate** or mediator / intercessor / helper when we **sin.** He is qualified to intercede for us because he is **righteous** and **he is the propitiation for our sins.** The word **propitiation** is the Greek ἱλασμός (hilasmos) and means an "appeasement necessitated by sin."[86] Some translations use the phrase "atoning sacrifice" here. The key is that the application parallels the purification offerings discussed earlier. Jesus' sacrifice provided the satisfaction of God's holy requirements as to our sin. Indeed, it is precisely because Jesus paid for our sins once and for all time (Hebrew 9:28) that fellowship is now

[85] William Arndt et al., *A Greek-English Lexicon of the New Testament,* 766.
[86] Ibid., 474.

possible. Observe that John used the present tense. John's focus was on the continuing work – he **is the propitiation for our sins** – that provides fellowship forgiveness and purification. While this is grounded in the historic reality of the cross, the benefit is now and continuing. We as Christians can confess our **sins** and enjoy forgiveness through the continuing ministry of our high priest and **advocate**, and no new animal offering is needed as under the Law Covenant because of Jesus' once for all time sacrifice that inaugurated the New Covenant.

Finally, note John's addition, **and not for ours only, but also for the sins of the whole world.** This is one of the many New Testament statements that explicitly undermines the Reform Theology concept of limited atonement—that Jesus died only for a small subset of humanity. (e.g., John 1:29; Hebrews 2:9) Those holding this view argue that if Jesus died for all, then *necessarily* all have been (or will be) saved. This supplants exegesis with philosophical reasoning. The conclusion rests on drawing inferences that are expressly rejected by the Bible, which repeatedly affirms both that (1) Jesus died for all people and (2) salvation is freely given only to those who put their trust in Christ. In his high priestly role, Jesus made the once for all sacrifice that was a propitiation for the entire world. This made it so that God, in His holiness, *could* exercise His prerogative to justify sinners, but He was never required to do so. That's why it is called grace. God has the sovereign right to extend or withhold mercy as He pleases (e.g., Romans 9), and by His grace and mercy God chooses to save those who have placed faith in Christ. This transaction is neither complicated nor ambiguous in the Bible.

Having said this, we should not view John's words that Jesus is **the propitiation...for the sins of the whole world** as gratuitous. Like much of what he wrote in First John, his words here were almost certainly against the backdrop of the lies of the deceivers he would later explicitly address. Even if Gnosticism was not yet formalized, it is difficult to deny that some of the ideas that were popularized in the second century were present in some form by the mid to late first century. We know that Gnostics were active in the early to mid-second century including persons like Saturninus, Basilides, and Velentinus. Important for our purposes, they saw themselves as Christians and as the elect having a secret knowledge no others had and no others could attain. As Antonia Triopolitis explains: "Thus, the Gnostics understood themselves as a 'chosen people,' an elite group, above the materially minded or unenlightened masses. Only a few of the sects called themselves Gnostics, 'the knowing ones.' The term was applied by the Christian heresiologists of the 2nd century C.E. to all who claimed to possess a special esoteric knowledge."[87] As he further explains concerning their rise to popularity in the second century:

> By the end of the 2nd century, Gnosticism had become a worldwide movement and a formidable foe to Christianity. Its members were an "elect" group who claimed to possess a secret knowledge or *gnosis* not available to the rest of the populace. This claim had a psychological appeal. It gave

---

[87] Antonía Tripolitis, *Religions of the Hellenistic-Roman Age* (Grand Rapids, MI; Cambridge, U.K.: William B. Eerdmans Publishing Company, 2002), 119–120.

the Gnostics a sense of security in an insecure world, and a sense of superiority. Through *gnosis*, they were released from the rule of Fate or Destiny, with its suffering and enslavement, and they knew that no matter what occurred, they would survive and that their ultimate destiny was union with the supreme Deity.[88]

The Gnostics believed only a small subset of humanity would be saved in the sense of receiving the gnosis, as Bingham explains: "The Gnostics had an elitist understanding of salvation; they divided humanity into two categories, the 'spiritual ones' who belong to the Father and the 'material ones' who belong to the Demiurge. As the 'spiritual ones,' the Gnostic believed, they were destined for salvation because of the divine spark within them (unlike the rest of humanity, who are asleep and have no hope)."[89] Of their development in the second century, Tripolitis makes the point that they considered themselves Christians: "Of the many gnostic sects that developed, the most important were those of Basilides (fl. ca. 130–150), Marcion (fl. 140–160), and Valentinus (fl. ca. 140–160). All three considered themselves Christians and claimed to preserve the true revelation of Christ."[90]

John's words about Jesus being **the propitiation...for the sins of the whole world** were not gratuitous. It is likely the

[88] Ibid., 141.
[89] D. Jeffrey Bingham, "One God, One Christ, One Salvation," *Christian History Magazine-Issue 96: The Gnostic Hunger for Secret Knowledge* (Carol Stream, IL: Christianity Today, 2007).
[90] Antonia Tripolitis, *Religions of the Hellenistic-Roman Age*, 125.

deceivers were claiming secret knowledge and a form of limited salvation because only the elect could attain the gnosis. Unfortunately, while Gnosticism died many of its ideas morphed into new groups with new labels, and some of that was fused into Christianity by Augustine and later by others. But in John's day he obviously saw the need, in no uncertain terms, to assert that Jesus died for all, not just for some or the elect.

Closing

I recognize this chapter is theologically heavy, but it is imperative that we not lose sight of how immensely practical it is. All of us should desire to walk in fellowship with our holy God and enjoy all the benefits of doing so. For that, we need to comprehend what fellowship means and how to experience it. As we will see, John had much more to say on the topic, but the material so far provides a good introduction. The challenge to all of us is to resolve that we want to walk in fellowship with God. This should be a priority, and that means that we take sin seriously and incorporate confession of known sins into our daily walk. Given our propensity to sin, you and I cannot possibly be in fellowship with God if confession of known sins is not a part of our walk. We need to let that sink in. The Old Testament believers under the Law understood this because of the purification and reparation offerings. We are New Covenant believers but God is still holy and fellowship still requires periodic foot washings to use the metaphor of John 13. If we are unwilling to confess known sins, we are walking in darkness. We need to resolve to put this epistle into practice and make confession a part of our walk.

Application Points

- MAIN PRINCIPLE: God is holy and our fellowship with Him is only possible if we walk in holiness and confess known sins as they occur, confident that God is faithful to forgive those sins and all unrighteousness based on the continuing vitality of the blood of Jesus Christ.

- In Jesus' high priestly he died as a propitiation for the sins of the world and he continues to serve as our advocate / intercessor / helper.

Discussion Questions

1. Assuming the statement that God is light means, or at least includes, the proposition that God is holy, how would you define holy?

2. What are some practical ramifications of God's holiness for our Christian walk?

3. John wrote that there is no darkness in God. Is darkness just sin or is there more to it?

4. If the concept of fellowship with God carries the idea of a mutual sharing of things in common, what is it that believers could share in common with God?

5. In practical terms, how can we develop a practice of confession of sins as a part of our walk with the Lord?

6. What are the implications of Jesus' sacrifice being a propitiation for the sins of the whole world?

Chapter 4

Knowing God

1 John 2:3-11

John opened his epistle with an eyewitness affirmation of the incarnation of Jesus Christ. In what most believe was approximately a three-and-a-half-year earthly ministry, John and the other apostles were as close to Jesus as anyone ever was. Some knew of Jesus by reputation. Others had heard him preach from the back of a large crowd. Still others had come face to face with him, and some had been miraculously healed. Perhaps any of these might have claimed to know Jesus. But there was a select group of people including the apostles and no doubt some others (like Lazarus and his sisters) that knew Jesus through extensive interaction and observation. They were closer to him than the others. They were his friends. They were blessed to have enjoyed this level of intimacy and could make the claim, "yes, I know Jesus," and they were not talking as some might of a casual acquaintance or single encounter. Jesus is not physically present with us today while we await his return, but the level of intimacy John experienced is available to those who walk in fellowship. Those who walk in the light can say, "yes, I know Jesus."

Outline

II. FELLOWSHIP MUST ACCORD WITH THE TRUTH-REALITY OF GOD'S HOLINESS AND MORAL PURITY (1:5-2:11)

a. Fellowship principles based on light and darkness (1:5-2:2)

b. Fellowship principles based on obedience and love (2:3-11)

i. Not keeping Jesus' commands means we do not know him, but through obedience we can know we abide in fellowship with him and that God's love is complete in us (2:3-6)

ii. The old command from the beginning of Jesus' earthly ministry to love one another is also a new command because the darkness is passing away and the true light is shining (2:7-8)

iii. Not loving the brethren means we are in the darkness, but when we love the brethren, we abide in the light (2:9-11)

Scripture and Comments

To this point, John introduced principles of fellowship through the lens of the nature of God. He is light and in Him is no darkness at all. Accordingly, the believer walking in fellowship must walk in the light and not the darkness. When a believer walks in the light, he or she enjoys fellowship with God. If the believer sins, restoration to fellowship requires confession and then God is just to forgive the confessed sin and all unrighteousness. This truth provides no license for intentional sin, but reflects Jesus' continuing high priestly role as our advocate / intercessor / helper. Next, we will see how John introduced further aspects of fellowship including knowing him, obedience to his commandments and word, perfected love, and abiding or remaining in him.

> **1 John 2:3** And hereby we do know that we know him, if we keep his commandments. **4** He that saith, I know him, and keepeth not his commandments, is a liar, and the truth is not in him. **5** But whoso keepeth his word, in him verily is the love of God perfected: hereby know we that we are in him. **6** He that saith he abideth in him ought himself also so to walk, even as he walked.

This is another of several passages in First John that have generated much debate that ultimately turns on the purpose of the epistle and the immediate contextual material about walking in the light. If John's purpose was to give a mixed group of genuine Christians and fake Christians "tests" to determine whether they are genuine Christians, then this verse teaches that the way you can **know** you are truly a Christian is by whether you **keep his commandments**. As I suggested in chapter 1, the tests for salvation view supplants genuine assurance based on God's promises with spurious assurance centered on human subjectivity and inevitable doubts. If this passage is a test for salvation, then a single violation of one of **his commandments** results in a failing grade and the test subject is not a child of God. Advocates for the tests for salvation view resist this result by arguing that it is only a continuing pattern of sin that would fail the test, but the language at hand is binary. It is a pass/fail test, and one infraction is a fail. This passage is better understood in the context of fellowship and walking in the light that was introduced in First John 1, and so provides additional aspects of fellowship, including experiencing intimacy with God and the love of God.

To understand what John was saying to his readers and by application to us, we begin with the word **know**. This is the Greek γινώσκω (ginōskō) and can have a range of meanings that include: "to arrive at a knowledge of someone or something,"[91] "to acquire information through some means,"[92] "to grasp the significance or meaning of something,"[93] and "to have sexual intercourse with."[94] This is similar to how "know" is used in English, where we might say we "know" a fact (e.g., George Washington was the first president) or that we "know" a person, but our meaning may be anything from someone we met once to a casual acquaintance to a close friendship. John used **know** in his Gospel to denote knowing someone with various levels of comprehension of who they are as a person: "the world knew him not" (1:10), "Jesus...knew all men" (2:24), "I am the good shepherd, and know my sheep, and am known of mine" (10:14), and "Father, the world hath not known thee: but I have known thee" (17:25). Of particular help to us is John's usage below:

> **John 14:6** Jesus saith unto him, I am the way, the truth, and the life: no man cometh unto the Father, but by me. 7 If ye had

---

91 William Arndt et al., *A Greek-English Lexicon of the New Testament*, 199.
92 Ibid., 200.
93 Ibid.
94 Ibid.

> known me, ye should have known my
> Father also: and from henceforth ye know
> him, and have seen him. **8** Philip saith unto
> him, Lord, shew us the Father, and it
> sufficeth us. **9** Jesus saith unto him, Have I
> been so long time with you, and yet hast
> thou not known me, Philip? he that hath
> seen me hath seen the Father; and how
> sayest thou *then*, Shew us the Father?

Here, we find Jesus saying that Philip had "not known" him. Obviously, Philip knew Jesus on one level but without a deeper comprehension that comes with a more intimate relationship. Jesus manifested God the Father in his incarnation, and Philip's words revealed he had not fully comprehended that. He had a distorted view of Jesus and in that sense did not yet **know** him. As Hodges explains: "I may *know* persons in the sense that I recognize them or am acquainted with them; but at the same time I may *not* know them in the sense of intimate knowledge or real perception of their character or nature."[95]

Jesus also taught his disciples that obedience demonstrates love for him, and in response to their obedience Jesus would reveal himself: "He that hath my commandments, and keepeth them, he it is that loveth me: and he that loveth me shall be loved of my Father, and I will love him, and will manifest myself to him." (John 14:21) It is this revealing of the Son in response to obedience that yields an experiential knowledge of the Son. Note that Jesus then added: "If a man love me, he will keep my words: and my Father will love him, and we will come unto him, and

---

[95] Zane Clark Hodges, *The Epistle of John: Walking in the Light of God's Love* (Irving, TX: Grace Evangelical Society, 1999), 77.

make our abode with him." (John 14:23) Jesus directly linked obedience to having the Father and the Son make their dwelling place with the believer, or in other words, experiencing fellowship. No doubt, John had these truths in mind when he wrote First John 2:3-5.

John wrote that **hereby we do know that we know him, if we keep his commandments.** The first **know** is a present tense verb denoting what we can know today. The second **know** is a perfect tense verb, denoting a past action with continuing consequences. Zane Hodges explains the perfect tense: "It is well to be reminded that the perfect tense 'is not a past tense but a present one, indicating not the past action as such but the present 'state of affairs' resulting from the past action' (Maximilian Zerwick, *Biblical Greek: Illustrated by Examples* [Rome: Scripta Pontificii Instituti Biblici, 1963], p. 96)."[96] Accordingly, we can **know** today that we previously came to an intimate and experiential knowledge of Jesus that continues to the present **if we keep his commandments.** Some mistakenly try to insert the Torah here, but John taught his readers (and us) what Jesus taught him. (*see* 1 John 1:1-5) It is Jesus' **commandments** at issue, and as we will see shortly, John especially had in mind the command to love one another as he loved them.

As we saw in First John 1:8-10, John elaborated first with a negative illustration, then a positive. The person who claims, **I know him, and keepeth not his commandments, is a liar.** (compare 1 John 1:6 and 1:10) John's logic was impeccable and indeed simple. If those who **know him...keep his commandments,** then it necessarily follows that those who do not **keep his commandments** do not

---

[96] Ibid.

know him, and thus their claim is a lie. Just as those that that "walk in darkness" do not "have fellowship with him," those that do not **keep his commandments** do not **know him**. Both of these passages are getting at the same practical reality of walking in the light and enjoying fellowship. How we live will betray whether we really do **know him** in the sense of an intimate and experiential knowledge or not. It is impossible to have that level of intimacy with **him** and not be changed. It is impossible to have that level of intimacy with **him** and not be in the light. Obviously, what John described surpassed academic knowledge. You can pass a theological exam in seminary withing knowing **him**.

Of the person falsely claiming to **know him** while not keeping **his commandments**, John also wrote that **the truth is not in him**. As addressed in the introductory material in chapter 1, John used **the truth** to refer more broadly to reality or some aspect of reality – what we might call **truth**-reality – centered on the person and works of God including his redemptive work through Jesus, who himself claimed to be "the truth." Up to this point, John explained that those who claim fellowship while walking in darkness "do not the truth" (1:6) and those that claim to "have no sin" do not have "the truth" in them (1:8). The point here, as before, is that the person making the false claim of knowing **him** has a distorted comprehension of **truth**-reality. That person's worldview is at odds with **the truth** and so they are deceived into believing they can have the intimacy that comes with fellowship but without obedience. Many Christians today believe this lie. As Christians, our choices have consequences.

On the positive side, he that **keepeth his** (Jesus') **word, in him verily is the love of God perfected**. (see also 1 John 4:12) The word **perfected** translates the Greek verb τελειόω (teleioō) and means to bring something to a state of completion. John's conclusion should come as no surprise based on Jesus' teachings:

> **John 13:34** A new commandment I give unto you, That ye love one another; as I have loved you, that ye also love one another. **35** By this shall all *men* know that ye are my disciples, if ye have love one to another.

> **John 15:12** This is my commandment, That ye love one another, as I have loved you.

> **John 15:17** These things I command you, that ye love one another.

Keeping Jesus' **commandments** includes the highest mandate we have of loving God and loving others, what James referred to in his epistle as the royal law. All other commands are an application or outworking of the command to love, and if love is not there neither is obedience in general. Therefore one who **keepeth his word** will experience **the love of God perfected** or completed in them. As will become apparent in First John 3:1-10, only those born again can love as Jesus loved, and exhibiting such love is what fellowship with God looks like to the observer. It is also confirming to the believer. We know we are eternally saved because of God's promises, but we **know that we are in him** in the sense of the vine and branches fellowship (see John 15:1-8) when God's **love** is **perfected** in us and flows out of us in our **love** for others. In fact, the person who claims to **abideth** or remain **in him**

86

(Jesus) **ought himself also so to walk, even as** Jesus **walked.** This matter of abiding will be addressed further in the notes on 2:24. Living in the light, living in fellowship, and abiding **in** Christ occur as we experience Christ in us and the power of Christ flowing through our lives. This is not always the Christian's experience, but it is the experience of those disciples connected to the vine, without whom we can do nothing. As Hodges notes, "The 'abider' is a believer who has learned to live like the Lord Jesus Christ."[97] This naturally leads to the question of how Jesus lived, which John addressed next.

> **1 John 2:7** Brethren, I write no new commandment unto you, but an old commandment which ye had from the beginning. The old commandment is the word which ye have heard from the beginning. **8** Again, a new commandment I write unto you, which thing is true in him and in you: because the darkness is past, and the true light now shineth.

Having just related a believer's keeping "his commandments" and "his word" to knowing Jesus and experiencing God's perfected love, John echoed Jesus' commandment from John 13:34-35. The **commandment** to love another is not **new** because Jesus taught it to the apostles, and John taught it to his readers. Indeed, for John's readers, this was **an old commandment which** they **had from the beginning** and **which** they **heard from the beginning.** The phrase **from the beginning** in First John 1:1 referred to the **beginning** of Jesus' earthly ministry. Here, it speaks to the **beginning** of the apostles' ministry—and

---

[97] Zane Clark Hodges, *The Epistle of John*, 83.

most assuredly John's ministry—to his readers. Yet at the same time John classified the **commandment** as something **new** that he is writing to them, **which thing is true in him** (Jesus) **and in you.** The word **true** translates the Greek adjective ἀληθής (alēthes) and in this context has the sense of being in accordance with fact or reality.[98] The truth of this **commandment** is grounded in it being a constituent part of the reality of who Jesus is.

John explained that the **commandment** was **new...because the darkness is past, and the true light now shineth.** The **commandment** is more than words on a page. It was **true in** Jesus because he made it reality in an absolute sense as he manifested God's love to the world (John 1:14; 1 John 1:2-3), and now it is **true in** John's readers because they manifest Jesus Christ and his love to the world. A new age began with the incarnation: "And the light shineth in darkness; and the darkness comprehended it not." (John 1:5) And again, "I have come a light into the world, that whosoever believeth on me should not abide in darkness." (John 12:46) As John's readers walked in the light (1 John 1:5) of fellowship with God and reflected Christ's love to the world, it may be said that **the darkness is past, and the true light now shineth.** John later wrote, "as he is, so are we in this world." (1 John 4:17)

> **1 John 2:9** He that saith he is in the light, and hateth his brother, is in darkness even until now. **10** He that loveth his brother abideth in the light, and there is none occasion of stumbling in him. **11** But he that hateth his brother is in darkness, and walketh in darkness, and knoweth not

---

98 William Arndt et al., *A Greek-English Lexicon of the New Testament*, 43.

whither he goeth, because that darkness hath blinded his eyes.

As already suggested above, the concepts of walking in the light, knowing Jesus in a close intimate way, abiding in him, and keeping his commandments, are all intertwined aspects of the same fellowship experience available to Christians. These verses relate these concepts back to the theological predicate for the entire epistle that John heard Jesus say: "that God is light, and in him is no darkness at all." (1 John 1:5)

Whereas John followed that predicate statement in First John 1:6 with a hypothetical claim to "have fellowship with him, and walk in darkness," here he related the same claim to the old/new commandment of First John 2:7-8 that we should love one another. (compare 1 John 3:11-15) If a Christian claims **he is in the light** but **hateth his brother** or fellow believer, in reality that Christian **is in darkness even until now**. Again, his logic is impeccable and simple. Because "God is light, and in him there is no darkness," it is impossible for the one who hates **his brother**, an action sourced in the **darkness**, to be **in the light**. This Christian believes he is experiencing the **light** and fellowship but in fact is experiencing **darkness** and distance, which John would later in his epistle refer to as death.

John now states the positive side of this reality—**he that loveth his brother abideth in the light**. This makes perfect sense as an application of First John 1:5 and leaves no gray area of retreat from John's binary doctrine. The Christian either **abideth in the light** or experiences **darkness**. Again we see John's favored term **abideth**, the Greek μένω (menō). (see 1 John 2:3-6) The Christian **that loveth his brother** is both abiding **in the light** and experiencing fellowship with the holy God. (1 John 1:6-7) Further, and building on the **light** imagery, John added that **there is none occasion of stumbling in him**. The phrase **occasion of** (or cause for) **stumbling** translates the Greek σκάνδαλον (skandalon) and its primary meaning is a trap. Other meanings are "an action or circumstance that leads one to act contrary to a proper course of action or set of beliefs"[99] and "that which causes offense or revulsion and results in opposition, disapproval, or hostility."[100] Because the context is abiding **in the light** and therefore being in fellowship with the holy God, the latter meaning is the best fit here. The metaphor is clear enough – one stumbles in the **darkness** not **in the light**. John's point was simply that the Christian abiding **in the light** had nothing **in him** that would cause God's disapproval. If that is so, we can infer that the Christian abiding **in the light** does not sin, a conclusion John made explicit later in his epistle. Here, as throughout the epistle, John introduced or implied issues he would address more fulsomely later.

Reverting back to the negative hypothetical, John expanded on the implications of hating one's **brother**. This Christian is not **in the light** as he falsely claims but is instead **in darkness, and walketh in darkness**. (compare 1 John 1:6) This Christian is not enjoying the intimate fellowship attendant to walking **in the light** nor is he guided by the old/new commandment. Rather, he faces the perils of walking **in darkness**, namely that he **knoweth not wither he goeth, because that darkness hath blinded his eyes**. Those in intimate fellowship with God are guided by their experiential knowledge of God (**the light**),

---

99 Ibid., 926.
100 Ibid.

which is reflected in how they relate to their fellow Christians. Those without such intimate fellowship with God reflect a lack of experiential knowledge of God in how they live, which looks no different than how lost people live because they are blindly stumbling about in the **darkness** like them. The blindness in view is the lack of experiential comprehension of the truth-reality that is unique to the sphere of **light**.

Closing

John's subunit on principles of fellowship ended where it began with a discussion of walking or abiding in the light. But as with nearly every unit of thought within the epistle, John introduced new issues while closing on others. John would write nothing more about the light explicitly, but in his final remarks he introduced by implication the idea that Christians do not sin while they are in fellowship with the holy God, and also connected fellowship with God and loving the brethren. These issues would be elaborated and lead to still further implications of living in the light. The challenge to us is why we would ever choose to stumble around in the darkness.

Application Points

- MAIN PRINCIPLE: We have assurance that we have come to know God intimately, abide in him, walk in the light, and have His perfected love in us when we keep His commandments and love the brethren, but disobedience and hate show we walk in darkness and the truth is not in us.

- When we obey the command to love our brethren, we are lights in this world.

Discussion Questions

1. In practical terms, what would be different in your life if you have a casual knowledge of Jesus Christ or an intimate knowledge of Jesus Christ?

2. Other than the command to love the brethren, what are some other of Jesus' commandments?

3. John wrote that the person that claims to know Jesus but doesn't keep His commandments is a liar. Why do you think John used such a strong term?

4. What are practical examples of how we can love our brethren or hate our brethren?

5. What are some examples of speech that shows we hate our brethren?

6. What are some examples of how we might think about a brother or sister that shows we hate them?

Chapter 5

Blessed Assurance

1 John 2:12-14

The antichrists were out in full force to sow doubts among John's readers in the same way Satan sowed doubt in Eve's mind by disputing the veracity of God's Word. The spiritual battle was being waged for the minds of God's people, and for John's friends. As the apostle Paul reminded the Ephesians: "For we wrestle not against flesh and blood, but against principalities, against powers, against the rulers of the darkness of this world, against spiritual wickedness in high places." (Ephesians 6:12) This war continues in our day and will continue until the Lord Jesus Christ returns and locks Satan away. Then and now the deceivers invariably attack the incarnation of the Son of God. They reject that God became flesh and dwelt among us. They mock the notion of the substitutionary atonement. They imbibe the most absurd claims of secularism but dismiss the resurrection out of hand. They package and re-package the same play book for each generation. That is why Paul warned the Ephesians against being "carried about with every wind of doctrine, by the sleight of men, and cunning craftiness, whereby they lie in wait to deceive." (Ephesians 4:14) In this milieu of mixed and confusing messages, John provided his readers a rich word of encouragement and assurance grounded in the reality the false teachers rejected. Even if his readers harbored doubts, John had no doubts whatsoever that they were not only genuine believers but overcomers. We can imagine those first century Christians hearing this beautiful epistle read aloud for the first time, perhaps sensing the foreboding overtones, then hearing such strong words of assurance. We can imagine the corporate sigh of relief and leap of joy in their hearts. This assurance was not only for them, but the Holy Spirit intended it for all of us who have also placed faith in Jesus Christ, the Son of God. We need to be encouraged daily as we live in a broken world with emissaries on mission to sow doubts while God implores us to reap grace.

Outline

III. ASSURANCE TO JOHN'S READERS AS OVERCOMERS (2:12-14)

    a. Their sins were forgiven (2:12)

    b. They know Jesus and have overcome the evil one (2:13)

    c. They know the Father and the Son, they are strong, God's Word abides in them and they have overcome the evil one (2:14)

Scripture and Comments

John completed a subunit (1:5-2:11) on principles of fellowship to lay the theological foundation for his readers before he addressed the occasion of his epistle, namely the antichrists or deceivers. Before turning to that, John assured his readers that they were not only children of God, but overcomers. They could withstand and overcome the deceivers and live for God despite all the challenges of living in the last hour.

> **1 John 2:12** I write unto you, little children, because your sins are forgiven you for his name's sake. **13** I write unto you, fathers, because ye have known him *that is* from the beginning. I write unto you, young men, because ye have overcome the wicked one. I write unto you, little children, because ye have known the Father. **14** I have written unto you, fathers, because ye have known him *that is* from the beginning. I have written unto you, young men, because ye are strong, and the word of God abideth in you, and ye have overcome the wicked one.

Any lingering presupposition that John was primarily concerned about fake believers self-deceived into thinking they were genuine Christians were laid to rest in these three verses. John's readers needed no "tests for salvation" because they had the promises of God (e.g., John 3:16) **and** the assurance of the apostle John who knew them and personally ministered to them. As previously noted, John's occasion for this epistle was not that his readers had fallen prey to the deceivers, nor that they were caught up in a serious sin problem or were fake Christians. In fact, John confirmed that they "know the truth." (1 John 2:21) The epistle coupled confirmation with caution. To this point, and by design, John had not explicitly referenced the deceivers. His approach had been to state the primary purpose of his writing (1 John 1:1-4) and set out the fundamental principles of fellowship that would produce confidence and victory. Before cautioning his readers about the deceivers, he encouraged them in the most emphatic terms by confirming his confidence in their walk with God. No doubt, John did this because the areas of John's confirmation were precisely the areas the deceivers would attack. It is ironic that so many misread this epistle to question the salvation of John's readers, thus aligning with what John expected from the deceivers. The epistle is not directed toward a wayward church or wayward Christians, but even solid churches and mature Christians can fall prey to the deceptions of the world and the devil.

These verses have sometimes been interpreted as dividing the audience into four groups – **little children** (2:12), **(little) children** (2:13), **young men** (2:13-14), and **fathers** (2:13-14) – based on their relative levels of maturity, but that is unlikely. The specific affirmations John assigned and the structure of those affirmations reflect a qualitative and cumulative assurance to all of his **little children**. To see this, the place to start is with what these four terms mean. John's opening reference in verse 12 to **little children** uses the Greek word τεκνίον (teknion), which he used repeatedly in the book to refer to all of his readers. (1 John 2:1, 2:28, 3:7, 3:18, 4:4, and 5:21) The word teknion means "little born ones"[101] and is the diminutive form of the Greek noun teknon, which refers to a biological child.[102]

[101] John F. Walvoord and Roy B. Zuck, Dallas Theological Seminary, *The Bible Knowledge Commentary: An Exposition of the Scriptures*, vol. 2 (Wheaton, IL: Victor Books, 1985), 886.

[102] Dougald McLaurin III, "Ancestry and Posterity," ed. Douglas Mangum et al., *Lexham Theological Wordbook*, Lexham Bible Reference Series (Bellingham, WA: Lexham Press, 2014).

Obviously they were not John's biological children. He selected this term for his readers because he viewed them as his spiritual offspring through his ministry in their lives. No doubt this expression was etched in John's mind because Jesus used it to refer to his apostles. (John 13:33) The **little children** in verse 13 is not the same Greek word translated **little children** in verse 12. Instead of teknion, he used παιδίον (paidion), which usually means "a child, normally below the age of puberty, *child*."[103] No one seriously argues that John was addressing readers who were literally pre-pubescent **children**. The words **young men** is the Greek νεανίσκος (neaniskos) and means "a relatively young man, *youth, young man*."[104] Just as there is no cause to take paidion to refer to pre-pubescent children, there is no reason to take **young men** in a literal biological sense. The word **fathers** is the Greek πατήρ (patēr) and can refer to a father or any biological ancestor (e.g., grandfather).[105] Just as John's use of **little children** (teknion) had a spiritual application, so also did the terms **children** (paidion), **young men** (neaniskos), and **fathers** (patēr).

Next, it is helpful to observe that John attributed a similar experience of knowledge to the **children** (**ye have known the Father**) and the **fathers** (**ye have known him that is from the beginning**). He likewise wrote that the **young men...have overcome the wicked one** and later that all of his "little children...have overcome" the deceivers. (1 John 4:4) This attribution of similar experiences to the **children**, **young men**, and **fathers** show that John's purpose was not say that some readers had attained to

---

[103] William Arndt et al., *A Greek-English Lexicon of the New Testament*, 749.
[104] Ibid., 667.
[105] Ibid., 787.

something the others had not. Rather, he encouraged all of his **little children** (teknion) based on their common experience of having God's Word in them, knowing the Father and the Son, and overcoming the devil. They were not three groups of believers with distinct experiences, but one group with common experiences John could qualitatively describe using the categories of **children, young men**, and **fathers**. Like **children** they stood in a close relationship with their heavenly **Father**. Like **young men** they were strong. Like **fathers** they had a mature understanding of the truth about the Son.

This understanding finds further support in the chiastic structure of the passage, which was a common Jewish writing device. In its simplest 1 2 2' 1' form, a chiasm may be defined as follows: "In a chiasm, elements one and four in one or more verses are parallel in thought, and points two and three are parallel in thought."[106] This structural device relates certain lines or passages together in a way that ascend to an apex or central point then descend in a way that reinforces what was previously said with similar or related statements. There are numerous instances of this in the Old Testament. Quite likely the Torah (Genesis through Deuteronomy) is chiastic with Leviticus at its center. The book of Lamentations is unquestionably structured as a chiasm, with chapters 1 and 5 corresponding, chapters 2 and 4 corresponding, and chapter 3 being the apex of the collection of lament poems. John's use here of a chiastic structure not only gives unity to the entire paragraph (2:12-14) but confirms its general application to all of his readers.

---

[106] Donald K. Campbell, "Foreword," in *Basic Bible Interpretation: A Practical Guide to Discovering Biblical Truth*, ed. Craig Bubeck Sr. (Colorado Springs, CO: David C. Cook, 1991), 138–139.

A little children, because your sins are forgiven you for his name's sake

B fathers, because ye have known him *that is* from the beginning

C young men, because ye have overcome the wicked one

C' little children, because ye have known the Father

B' fathers, because ye have known him *that is* from the beginning

A' young men, because ye are strong, and the word of God abideth in you, and ye have overcome the wicked one

John's first statement (A) emphatically affirmed his belief that all of his readers were Christians: **I write unto you, little children, because your sins are forgiven you for his name's sake**. The reference to **his** almost certainly refers to Jesus, who John just referenced in 2:6 and 8. Also, the reference to forgiveness implicated Jesus' work on the cross. This was consistent with John's other references to "his name":

> **John 1:12** But as many as received him, to them gave he power to become the sons of God, *even* to them that believe on his name:

> **John 20:31** But these are written, that ye might believe that Jesus is the Christ, the Son of God; and that believing ye might have life through his name.

We should not understand **name** to signify the word "Jesus," a common first century name for Jewish males.

Rather, **his name** refers to Jesus' person, works, and exalted status, for which he is known or has a reputation. Here, it is what Jesus accomplished at Calvary when he said, "It is finished." (John 19:30)

John twice addressed his readers as **fathers** (B and B'), affirming that they **have known him that is from the beginning.** This repetition gives strong confirmation of the chiastic pattern, which John may well have used to aid in memorization of the many beautiful truths packed in First John 2:12-14. The descriptor **fathers** suggests being well-grounded in the truth such that they could instruct others. The phrase **have known** translates the perfect tense of γινώσκω (ginōskō) previously addressed in the notes to First John 2:3 ("hereby we do know that we know him"). As noted there, this tense indicates a present state that began in the past. John's statement undoubtedly looked back to the immediately preceding material in First John 2:3-11 to remove any potential misunderstanding that John doubted whether his readers "know Jesus" in the sense of experiencing close intimate fellowship with **him**. As is frequently the case, John's use of the pronoun **him** could be taken in more than one way, but given the immediately preceding references in 2:6, 8, and 12, and John's specific use of **the Father** elsewhere in the chiasm, it is probable the reference here is to Jesus. More difficult is the expression **from the beginning.** Often, interpreters want words and phrases to have fixed meanings, but that is not how language works. Many words and phrases have a range of meanings and context is determinative. I suggested that **from the beginning** meant the beginning of Jesus' earthly ministry in First John 1:1 with its obvious focus on the incarnation. I suggested the same phrase meant the beginning of his readers' Christian walk in First John 2:7

because of the focus on their receipt of the commandment to love the brethren. Here, **from the beginning** relates a fact about Jesus and is best understood to refer to his presence at creation. (compare John 1:1)

In the first part of the apex of his chiasm (C), John called his readers **young men**, which suggests strength and vigor. With such qualities, John affirmed his readers **have overcome the wicked one**. The Greek verb νικάω (nikaō) translated **overcome** means "to win in the face of obstacles, *be victor, conquer, overcome, prevail.*"[107] John used the perfect tense indicating a past victory and present status as conquerors or victors. John would later confirm that as God's children they have all "overcometh the world: and this is the victory that overcometh the world, even our faith." (1 John 5:4) The **wicked one** refers to Satan or the devil. (1 John 3:8, 10) John referenced the **wicked one** again in First John 3:12 and 5:18-19. The natural question is, in what sense were his readers victors over the devil? No doubt, the devil was behind the work of the deceivers that John had not yet explicitly addressed. But as we will see, the deceivers deny the reality of the incarnation and that Jesus is the Christ. In view of the structure of the passage (see A and A' above), the victory in view was their faith in Jesus' **name** that was not only the basis for their **sins** being **forgiven** but also the fellowship they enjoyed. Jesus' **name** is grounded in the incarnation that led to the cross, and the deceivers rejected all of that.

John's statements in (C) and (C') together form the apex, coupling their strength as victors with their knowledge of **the Father**. John referred to his readers as **(little) children** or paidion, but not to reflect youth or immaturity. John no

---

[107] William Arndt et al., *A Greek-English Lexicon of the New Testament*, 673.

doubt recalled that after the resurrection, Jesus addressed the eleven as his "children" (paidion), reflecting his role in nurturing and instructing them. (John 21:5) John's readers were now the **children** who received John's nurture and instruction in the truth. As a result, they **have known the Father**. The verb **known** is the perfect tense of the now familiar *ginōskō* that reflects their close, intimate knowing of and fellowship with God **the Father**. Combined with the repeated statements that his readers (B and B') **have known him that is from the beginning**, the cumulative assurance was that his readers enjoyed fellowship with **the Father** and the Son. (compare 1 John 1:3)

Finally, closing the chiasm (A'), John addressed his readers again as **young men** because they **are strong, and the word of God abideth in you, and ye have overcome the wicked one**. Within the chiasm, these affirmations (A') paralleled the affirmation to the **little children** (A), confirming John's assurance that his readers were all overcomers. The word **strong** translates the Greek ἰσχυρός (ischyros) and means "being strong physically, mentally, or spiritually."[108] John's affirmation that they **are strong** is nowhere else repeated in the epistle, but it provided encouragement that they could withstand the deceivers he would warn them about. It was not only that they **have overcome** (perfect tense) **the wicked one**, but that John was confident in how they would face the present peril. Finally, John noted that **the word of God abideth** in them. John's chiasm of affirmations looked back to the immediately preceding material in First John 2:3-11 where John addressed keeping God's **word** and having the truth in them. Here, John affirmed his belief that his readers

---

[108] Ibid., 483.

had God's **word** abiding in them. It is not just that they knew God's **word** but that it functioned as their spiritual DNA guiding their lives. They had a right view of reality grounded in the truth, which was diametrically opposed to the doctrine of the deceivers.

Closing

The more I study the Bible the more I find myself contemplating passages I once thought were simple but now find profound. Professor Harry Leafe always told his students (including me) that maturity is not always about learning more Bible, but coming to a better understanding of the implications of truths we already know. Surely First John 2:12-14 falls into that category for me. It is like a gift that, once opened and examined, will never fit back in the box again. If we have what John believed of his readers – if we walk in the light – then we can apply these affirmations to ourselves. We have come to know the Father and the Son. We have overcome the evil one. God's Word abides in us. These are transformative truths.

Application Points

MAIN PRINCIPLE: Believers that walk in the light of fellowship with God are strong, have come to know the Father and the Son intimately, have overcome the evil one, and have God abiding in them.

Discussion Questions

1. Why do you think, from the context of the epistle, that John referred to his readers in verse 12 as little children then confirmed their sins are forgiven?

2. What are some implications for us if we have overcome the evil one?

3. Can Christians be attacked or deceived by Satan?

4. How does Satan operate and what are his primary goals regarding Christians?

5. What does it mean to have God's Word abiding in us? Is that the same or different than knowing God's Word, memorizing God's Word, or understanding God's Word?

6. What is the relationship between spiritual maturity and having God's Word abiding in us?

Chapter 6

Danger and Deception

1 John 2:15-27

There are two prevalent extremes among Christians. At one end of the continuum are those that see the devil behind every corner and every few years pick a new antichrist (often the candidate they are not voting for). Everything is a conspiracy and they are the only ones clever enough to see it. At the other end are those that don't believe in the devil or else believe his existence isn't relevant to their lives. The truth presented in the Bible lies somewhere between the extremes. My observation is that, even among those that recognize Satan is real, the extent of his deception is probably not fully realized. The Bible says that our "adversary the devil, as a roaring lion, walketh about, seeking whom he may devour." (1 Peter 5:8) We are warned against being deceived (Colossians 2:8) and exhorted to suit up for the spiritual battle before us (Ephesians 6:10-18). John wrote that we know the "whole world lieth in" the control of the evil one. (1 John 5:19) As Christians seeking to grow and enjoy fellowship with God, we need a Biblical understanding of the dangers posed by the allures of the world system and the deceptions of Satan who can be "transformed into an angel of light" (2 Corinthians 11:14) and speak through deceivers claiming to speak truth. John warned his readers, and by application warned us, of the dangers and deceptions, but also provided instruction for discerning truth and lies.

Outline

IV. WARNINGS ABOUT LIVING IN THE LAST HOUR (2:15-27)

   a. Warning about the allures of the world system (2:15-17)

      i. Love of the world system is incompatible with God's love in us as a controlling influence (2:15)

      ii. The allures of the world system are from the world not God (2:16)

      iii. The world system and its allures are passing away but the one that does God's will abides forever (2:17)

   b. Warning about the antichrists that deny truth in the last hour (2:18-23)

      i. It is the last hour and many antichrists have come who were with the apostles but not in fellowship with them (2:18-19)

      ii. Interim Purpose Statement: That they know the truth-reality and that no lie originates from the truth-reality (2:20-21)

      iii. The antichrists (deceivers) deny the truth-reality about the Father and the Son (2:22-23)

  c. Exhortation to hold to the truth-reality and abide in the Father and the Son (2:24- 27)

      i. If the truth-reality abides in you, you will abide in the Father and the Son (2:24-25)

      ii. <u>Interim Purpose Statement</u>: To warn his readers about the deceivers (2:26)

      iii. His readers have the anointing from God, and so do not need to learn from the deceivers, but to continue abiding in fellowship with God (2:27)

<u>Scripture and Comments</u>

John opened his epistle with an eyewitness verification of the incarnation of the Son of God and the profound concept of fellowship with the Father and the Son. This doorway opened to the truths he wanted to convey to his readers about fellowship, knowing God, abiding in God, and mature love for the brethren. John also knew that personal choices, the allures of the world, and the deceptions of the evil one all posed serious dangers to his readers' spiritual walks. After affirming his readers in 2:12-14, John transitioned to the warnings and exhortations concerning the world and its teachers that occasioned the writing of his epistle.

> **1 John 2:15** Love not the world, neither the things *that are* in the world. If any man love the world, the love of the Father is not in him. **16** For all that *is* in the world, the lust

of the flesh, and the lust of the eyes, and the pride of life, is not of the Father, but is of the world. 17 And the world passeth away, and the lust thereof: but he that doeth the will of God abideth for ever.

From John's perspective, walking in fellowship with God is incompatible with loving **the world** and **the things that are in the world**. The term **world** occurs frequently in John's writings and translates the Greek κόσμος (kosmos), which can refer to all people (e.g., John 3:16), but in this context has the meaning of "the sum total of everything here and now."[109] This is not only the material things of the **world** system and its inhabitants, but also its biases, prejudices, philosophies, pursuits, religions, and more. As John later commented, "we know that we are of God, and the whole world lieth in wickedness." (1 John 5:19) The translation "wickedness" is elsewhere translated "wicked one" (e.g., 1 John 2:13-14) and the point of First John 5:19 is that the world is under Satan's influence and power. For this reason, **the world** system and all it contains is corrupted and Christians are not to **love the world** system.

Often this passage is construed narrowly to warn against centering one's life on pursuing money and the things it can buy, but it says a great deal more. At the Fall, Eve was tempted not just to eat the forbidden fruit but to accept Satan's lie that "your eyes shall be opened, and ye shall be as gods, knowing good and evil." (Genesis 3:5) Generally speaking, the material things of the **world** are amoral. That is, they are not in themselves sinful. Rather, it is our response to those things, the priority we place on those things, and what we are willing to do in the pursuit of

109 William Arndt et al., *A Greek-English Lexicon of the New Testament*, 561.

those things, that is sin. But more than that, Eve was told she would not need God in her life because "ye shall be as gods." The secularism Satan peddled to humanity has given birth to a host of beliefs and philosophies that exclude God (e.g., 2 Corinthians 10:3-5; Colossians 2:8), including methodological materialism and naturalism that would explain everything, including the origin of the universe and life, from purely random and unguided natural causes. In the United States, we have invested billions of dollars indoctrinating our children with these ideas while scratching our heads in disbelief at what we reaped. Too many Christians believe they can play with fire by taking in what **the world** offers and still enjoy fellowship with God. As throughout his epistle, John's binary theology in this passage left no room for compromise. When we pursue a piece of **the world** we get the corrupted secularism behind it, and that accomplishes in our lives what Satan designed it to accomplish.

John added that **if any man love the world, the love of the Father is not in him**. Recall that John already stated that "whoso keepeth his word, in him verily is the love of God perfected: hereby know we that we are in him." (1 John 2:5) There and here, John's point was that fellowship with God (walking in the light, 1 John 1:5) requires keeping His word so that we experience the perfecting or bringing to completion of the **love of** God in us. To **love the world** and its allures is antithetical to experiencing the perfected **love of the Father** in us because **the world** is founded on an entirely different set of principles, priorities, and philosophies. The Christian in **love** with **the world** does not experience the power of the **love of the Father...in him** as the very DNA of his or her thoughts, words, and actions. More than anything, churches in the United

States today are weak because we want a little bit of God and the allures of **the world** at the same time, then struggle to comprehend why we don't feel close to God and why our lives don't reflect **the love of the Father** to others. Recall that Satan offered Jesus the kingdoms of **the world** if only Jesus would worship him. (Matthew 4:8-10) What price will we have to pay for indulging in **the world**?

John elaborated on the foolishness of compromise with **the world**. As he explained, **all that is in the world, the lust of the flesh, and the lust of the eyes, and the pride of life, is not of the Father, but is of the world**. It is a part of our fallen nature to crave the things **of the world**—to seek fulfillment from the creation rather than the Creator. We have physical desires or see something we want that God says is off limits or load up on the new bestselling self-help book. We convince ourselves what we desire will make us happy, and perhaps tell ourselves God is all about our happiness. We convince ourselves that what we "feel" or "desire" is who we are as persons, and we cannot be wrong for who we are, i.e., for how God made us, and so we pursue what we crave. Our thinking supplants God's Word and shouts in defiance that we know best, and by implication that God's provision for the moment is inadequate.

The **lust** or desire **of the flesh** concerns our thought life. We cannot limit this to a single category like sexual craving because our fallen nature is comprehensively tainted. The apostle Paul outlined the severity of our condition in Romans 1, showing that in our fallen nature we suppress truth and change the truth into lies, worship the creation, have senseless uncritical thinking, darkened hearts, and abased minds. Commensurate with the scope of our fallenness and its impact in our hearts and minds is the scope of our wicked thinking and desires, which is why Paul exhorted the believers in Rome to renew their minds. (Romans 12:1-2) These desires are sourced in **the world** system and not the light, and to embrace worldly thinking is to step out of the light into the darkness of **the world**. Especially dangerous is the secularized mindset of **the world** that tells us **the world** "is all that is or was or ever will be," to borrow Carl Sagan's atheistic mantra about the cosmos. Our fallen nature is prone to thinking what we need most is available in **the world** and will satisfy, which of course is a lie. The **lust of the eyes** speaks directly to covetousness as we desire what we see. This, of course, need not be visually seen, as our mind's eye is adept at creating fantasies to fan the flames of our deepest desires. The lie is that we need what our **eyes** desire, we deserve what our **eyes** desire, and we must have at all costs what our **eyes** desire. The root problem is not that God failed to provide sufficiently, but our own **pride of life**. The word **life** is the Greek βίος (bios) and is not merely being alive but the activities associated with one's life and the resources used to maintain it.[110] These desires have a way of puffing us up in our own thinking and twisting our minds in such a way that re-prioritizes our lives.

The foolishness of pursuing the world is confirmed in the temporariness of the **world** which is passing **away, and the lust thereof**. In other words, the **world** and all its allures that so captivate our hearts will soon be gone forever. The choice John put to his readers was between temporary gratification and eternal blessings. A wise preacher I know said that if we could see in the moment of decision the future costs of our decision, how often we would choose

---

[110] Ibid., 177.

better. If we could see in that moment how our consenting decision or victimless crime will affect us and those closest to us, perhaps we would choose better. But too often we walk by sight and not by faith, and this leads inexorably to ruin.

In contrast to the temporary nature of **the world...he that doeth the will of God abideth forever.** The Christian in fellowship with God experiences the perfected **love of the Father** and does not fade **away** with **the world,** but remains or abides **forever.** This is not a statement about how to obtain, maintain or validate eternal life, but rather a promise about the consequences of living in fellowship with God. John introduced a concept he developed later in the epistle (1 John 2:28, 4:17-18) about a day of judgment or evaluation for Christians where our faithfulness will be rewarded. The contrast in First John 2:17 is between a life that obtains only the temporary scraps of **the world** and a transformed life that obtains permanent treasure in heaven by experiencing the perfected **love of the Father.** This transformed life characterized by **love** can be experienced now and will transcend the passing away of **the world** as we are commended and rewarded by Jesus Christ in the day of judgment.

> **1 John 2:18** Little children, it is the last time: and as ye have heard that antichrist shall come, even now are there many antichrists; whereby we know that it is the last time. **19** They went out from us, but they were not of us; for if they had been of us, they would *no doubt* have continued with us: but *they went out*, that they might be made manifest that they were not all of us.

John warned his readers about the world system and then turned to its emissaries who sought to undermine truth and distort reality. With his favorite term of endearment to those he ministered to, John addressed his **little children** and warned that **it is the last time**. A more literal translation is **the last** hour, but the point is not a literal hour or even a short moment in time, but the culminating age. We have many New Testament reference to the **last** days, hour, or time. (Acts 2:17; 2 Timothy 3:1; Hebrews 1:2; James 5:3; 1 Peter 1:20; 2 Peter 3:3; Jude 18) These expressions indicate the final stage of human history preceding the return of Christ, and this is the period in which we presently live.

The **last time** is and will continue to be characterized by a succession of **antichrists** that will culminate in *the* **antichrist**. The word **antichrist** is the Greek ἀντίχριστος (antikristos) meaning an adversary or enemy of the Messiah, and only occurs in First and Second John. The person that will be *the* **antichrist** is the subject of many passages outside of John's writings such as Daniel 7:8-9 (the "little horn"), 2 Thessalonians 2:1-12 (the "son of perdition"), and Revelation 13 (the "beast...out of the sea"). I will not further delve into the person and work of the **antichrist** that is to come as that goes beyond John's warning here. The crucial point John made was that the deceptive methods of the **antichrist** to come were already at work. John would have his readers (and us) understand that **even now are there many antichrists; whereby we know that it is the last time**. The age in which John's readers lived, and in which we now live, is characterized by the prevalence of **antichrists**. While John did not itemize the false doctrines the **antichrists** sought to proliferate, the moniker John applied to them describes their purpose—to undermine the person and work of Jesus Christ. But if Jesus is the truth and perfectly declared the Father, then the **antichrists** were necessarily anti-truth. They sowed the ideology of darkness and were at war with the truth and light. They were proponents of a counter-reality, and we should not presume their lies were limited to denying the incarnation or certain Christian beliefs. They were deceivers of the first order, and John's readers lived in an age of deception and we do as well. The apostle Paul wrote: "But evil men and seducers shall wax worse and worse, deceiving, and being deceived." (2 Timothy 3:13)

John explained that the **antichrists...went out from us, but they were not of us.** At one point the deceivers were with John and other believers and perhaps other apostles, but they were **not of us**, meaning they did not have "fellowship with us" like John wanted with his readers. (1 John 1:3) Recalling that fellowship entails sharing things in common, John's words beg the question of what the deceivers did not share in common with **us**. John later explained that the deceivers denied Jesus (2:23) and did not confess that Jesus Christ is come in the flesh (4:2-3). In fact, John continued, **if they had been of us**, i.e., in fellowship with John and the others about the person and work of the Son of God, **they would no doubt have continued with us: but they went out, that they might be made manifest that they were not all of us.** While our works do not falsify a claim to be a Christian, they can falsify a claim to fellowship with those who remained steadfast to apostolic doctrine. The deceivers left John and the others because of disagreements about Jesus and the incarnation, and thus proved their lack of fellowship with John and also with the Father and the Son. (1 John 1:3) The word **manifest** is phaneroō that John used in 1:2

to describe how in the incarnation Jesus "manifested" eternal life. In the same way, the actions of the **antichrists** made their true colors visibly apparent to all.

A natural question to ask at this point concerns the identity of the **antichrists**. We may safely assume that their identity was commonly known to John's readers and so did not require further identification. It is likely that the deceivers self-identified as Christians and not by another label, and as John confirmed, they had been with him and perhaps other apostles for some length of time before breaking away. Attempts to identify a specific leader of the **antichrists** or to assign a specific label have not reached a consensus. Moreover, if there had been a label or leading figure John could have identified, doing so might have diminished the staying power of the epistle. Modern readers might set it aside as an irrelevant polemic against persons who have not posed a danger to apostolic Christianity for many centuries. John, and more pointedly the Holy Spirit, must have known that after the present **antichrists** were gone others would come. The personalities and labels would change but not the methodology and motives, and certainly not the target of their lies. From this perspective, the wisdom of John's approach was sound.

What we can safely say is that in their denial of the incarnation, the deceivers reflected beliefs seen among contemporary persons and groups in the first century and later. Cerinthus (AD 50-100) might be labeled as an early Gnostic who taught that Christ entered a human named Jesus at his baptism, empowered miracles, but abandoned Jesus before the crucifixion. Church tradition suggests Cerinthus opposed John. A view known as Docetism denied the incarnation by arguing that Jesus was not actually corporeal and that his human form was an illusion. This view was certainly present during the second century, and insipient forms may have been present in the first. Similarly, by the late first century Gnosticism was beginning to formalize, and it flourished by the mid-second century with leaders like Basilides and Valentinus. Their beliefs were complex and multifaceted but among other things held that what is material is evil and the true Christ was not the human Jesus but instead "unite[d] with the man Jesus (either at his conception or at his baptism) to bring mankind the saving knowledge ('gnosis') of its true origin and destiny" then abandoned Jesus before the crucifixion.[111] At the end of the day, whatever the label, we need to guard ourselves against those that through whatever clever means diminish or deny the incarnation. Whatever they call themselves, they are **antichrists**.

> **1 John 2:20** But ye have an unction from the Holy One, and ye know all things. **21** I have not written unto you because ye know not the truth, but because ye know it, and that no lie is of the truth. **22** Who is a liar but he that denieth that Jesus is the Christ? He is antichrist, that denieth the Father and the Son. **23** Whosoever denieth the Son, the same hath not the Father: *(but) he that acknowledgeth the Son hath the Father also.*

Having warned his readers about the world system and the deceivers who reject truth, John encouraged and confirmed his readers. Deceivers always claim some bit of

---

[111] F. L. Cross and Elizabeth A. Livingstone, eds., *The Oxford Dictionary of the Christian Church* (Oxford; New York: Oxford University Press, 2005), 1688.

secret knowledge. Satan did that in the Garden when he dialogued with Eve, the Gnostics taught that the secret knowledge of gnosis was only available to a select group (see notes on 1 John 2:2), and deceivers today do the same. The primary reason they obtain a stronghold among Christians is because of Biblical illiteracy and perhaps also an ignorance of history that might otherwise reveal that what appears new is just old lies repackaged. In any event, the deceivers in John's day had nothing to offer his readers because his readers had **an unction from the Holy One**. The archaic term **unction** is the Greek noun χρῖσμα (chrisma) and usually means anointing or anointing oil. In the Septuagint, the Greek translation of the Old Testament, this Greek word is used for anointing oil (e.g., Exodus 29:7, 30:25) or anointing (e.g., Exodus 40:15), and is used once of the anointed one or Messiah (Daniel 9:26). In the present text, it is not a literal anointing with oil that is in view. Much of what John wrote about in his epistle was rooted in Jesus' teachings from John 13-16. Jesus told the eleven:

> **John 14:16** And I will pray the Father, and he shall give you another Comforter, that he may abide with you for ever; **17** *Even* the Spirit of truth; whom the world cannot receive, because it seeth him not, neither knoweth him: but ye know him; for he dwelleth with you, and shall be in you.

> **John 16:13** Howbeit when he, the Spirit of truth, is come, he will guide you into all truth: for he shall not speak of himself; but whatsoever he shall hear, *that* shall he speak: and he will shew you things to come.

Anointing with oil typically symbolized the presence of God. That Jesus promised his disciples the Holy Spirit of truth would dwell in them is the anointing. What John explained to his readers is that Jesus, the **Holy One**, provided them the Holy Spirit, and as a result, they **know all things**. John did not mean they **know** everything there is to know. Rather, they **know** the truth declared by Jesus and passed to them through John and the apostles, and that has always been and remains the great antidote against the world's lies. Recall that the truth is not just some true propositions but the truth-reality grounded in the person of God including His redemptive plan. This truth-reality was perfectly declared by the Son in his incarnation, who claimed to be "the truth." (John 14:6) The world's lies are always contrary to the truth-reality.

That which denies the truth is a lie. John posed his response to the deceivers as a question: **Who is a liar but he that denieth that Jesus is the Christ?** Not only was such a denial contrary to the truth, grounded in historic fact, but it exposed such a person as an **antichrist that denieth** reality concerning the **Father and the Son**. It is not possible to deny the one without denying the other. Indeed, **whosoever denieth the Son** – whoever denies **that Jesus is the Christ** – does not have any part of **the Father**. This is unsurprising as Jesus taught that "no man cometh unto the Father, but by me." (John 14:6)

> **1 John 2:24** Let that therefore abide in you, which ye have heard from the beginning. If that which ye have heard from the beginning shall remain in you, ye also shall continue in the Son, and in the Father. **25** And this is the promise that he hath promised us, *even* eternal life.

Having encouraged his readers that they have the Holy Spirit and know the truth, John exhorted them to **let that therefore abide in you, which ye have heard from the beginning.** The Greek verb translated **abide** is μένω (menō) and means to continue or remain in a place. Here, what they **heard from the beginning,** meaning what they **heard** from John and the apostles and perhaps others when they first became Christians, should **abide in** them as the foundation or worldview on which they think and live. This is the same "truth" that they already knew as John confirmed in First John 2:21. As Hodges explains, holding fast to the truth they already possessed "is the way that the readers will in fact triumph over the wicked one's agents, the antichrists."[112]

If the truth they had **from the beginning** of their Christian walks continued to **abide** or **remain in** them, the result would be that they **shall continue** (i.e., abide or remain) **in the Son, and in the Father.** The key then to abiding in **the Son** and **the Father** is having God's truth **abiding** in us. This matter of abiding is another facet of fellowship, a primary topic from the beginning of the epistle. In addressing the issue of abiding, John built on what Jesus taught him and the other disciples (not Judas Iscariot) in John 15.

> **John 15:1** I am the true vine, and my Father is the husbandman. **2** Every branch in me that beareth not fruit he taketh away: and every *branch* that beareth fruit, he purgeth it, that it may bring forth more fruit. **3** Now ye are clean through the word which I have spoken unto you. **4 Abide** in me, and I in you. As the branch cannot bear fruit of itself,

---

[112] Zane Clark Hodges, *The Epistle of John*, 114.

except it **abide** in the vine; no more can ye, except ye **abide** in me. 5 I am the vine, ye *are* the branches: He that **abideth** in me, and I in him, the same bringeth forth much fruit: for without me ye can do nothing. 6 If a man **abide** not in me, he is cast forth as a branch, and is withered; and men gather them, and cast *them* into the fire, and they are burned. 7 If ye **abide** in me, and my words abide in you, ye shall ask what ye will, and it shall be done unto you. 8 Herein is my Father glorified, that ye bear much fruit; so shall ye be my disciples.

It is not my purpose to provide a fulsome exegesis of John 15:1-8, but it will serve our purposes to make some observations because this passage underlays much of First John. Jesus provided teaching only to the eleven. Nothing in this passage is about evangelism or whether someone is a genuine believer because Jesus expressly stated they "are clean through the word which I have spoken unto you." (John 15:3) Instead, the teaching was directed to the eleven as believers exhorting them to abide in him, with the promise that he would abide in them, and as a result they would be fruitful. This is a discipleship or sanctification passage. Because all the branches begin in Christ (John 15:2), the metaphor is about believers. Continuing the metaphor, if a branch / believer is not fruitful, the branch is lifted up higher on the trellis to get more light in the hope that it will become fruitful. The translation in verse 2 "taketh away" is of a Greek word that has the primary meaning of "to raise to a higher place or position,"[113] which comports with what we know of ancient viticulture and

---

[113] William Arndt et al., *A Greek-English Lexicon of the New Testament*, 28.

with common sense. Unfruitful vines were typically lower on the trellis and were lifted higher to receive more light. Fruitful vines / believers are pruned to become even more fruitful. But if a believer chooses not to abide in Jesus, he is a Christian that refuses to be a disciple, he will not bear fruit, and his unfruitfulness is metaphorically described as a discarded vine. (John 15:6) Jesus expressly connected the concept of his disciples abiding in him with his words abiding in them. (John 15:7)

Turning back to First John, he added that **this is the promise that he hath promised us, even eternal life.** John and his readers have **eternal life**, not because of their works but because God **promised** it. Yet the deceivers denied the Father and the Son (e.g., 1 John 2:22) and so struck at the foundation of what they **heard from the beginning.** This should have raised all kinds of red flags for John's readers.

> **1 John 2:26** These *things* have I written unto you concerning them that seduce you. **27** But the anointing which ye have received of him abideth in you, and ye need not that any man teach you: but as the same anointing teacheth you of all things, and is truth, and is no lie, and even as it hath taught you, ye shall abide in him.

This is another interim purpose statement in the epistle (compare 2:1-2). This was not intended to characterize the entire epistle. John wrote **these things...concerning them that seduce you**, a clear reference to the immediately preceding material (1 John 2:12-25) about the deceivers (anti-christs). The word **seduce** translates the Greek verb πλανάω (planaō) and means to mislead or deceive or lead astray, which is why I have referred to these false teachers as deceivers. It is apparent the deceivers wanted to mislead John's readers about whether Jesus was the Christ (see 1 John 2:22) and whether he could provide eternal life (1 John 2:25), which John assured his readers they had.

John again confirmed and encouraged his readers. The **anointing which** they **received of him** – that we previously identified as the Holy Spirit – **abideth** or continued in them. The pronoun **him** likely refers to Jesus, who promised to send the Holy Spirit. John readers did not **need...that any man teach** them because **the same anointing teacheth** them **all things, and is truth, and is no lie.** This verse should not be misconstrued as a statement against learning about the word of God from other people, for otherwise, John would invalidate his own teaching ministry. Rather, the issue is the source of the doctrine. His point was that they did not need teaching sourced in **man** when they could learn of the Spirit. From John's perspective, a person could speak doctrine sourced in the Holy Spirit or sourced in the world, a point he took up later in the epistle. (see 1 John 4:1-6)

Closing

As Christians, the world system and its emissaries have nothing we need. Yet it tugs at us through our own internal lust patterns, preys upon us with its allures, and persuades us through deception. If anything, we probably underestimate the dangers. Our culture is so saturated with the ideologies and allures of the world that we can begin to breathe its air and drink its water without realizing it. Satan does not have to yank us into the darkness in an instant. He is far more likely to try to set us on a slow drift at such an incremental pace that it may seem we are not moving at all. Yet with the passage of time, as if we'd fallen asleep in a boat and awakened miles from where we started, we can find ourselves stumbling around in the dark and possibly deceiving ourselves about the whole thing. The solution, according to the apostle, was to let the apostolic doctrine (now found in the New Testament) abide in us as a guiding and controlling influence so that we will abide in fellowship with the Father and the Son. This speaks of constancy and vigilance that is more likely when we are aware of the dangers. The apostle Peter wrote that "the end of all things is at hand: be ye therefore sober, and watch unto prayer." (1 Peter 4:7)

Application Points

- MAIN PRINCIPLE: As believers we need to be self-aware of our own unredeemed nature and its potential to crave the things of the world and believe the deceptions of the world and its emissaries who oppose God and spread lies, knowing that if we let God's Word abide in us, we will abide in the Father and the Son.

- Christians do not need the world's teachings because we have the anointing of the Holy Spirit.

Discussion Questions

1. John anticipates that Christians can have lusts or internal desires for the things of the world. Where do those desires come from?

2. What are some widespread deceptions or flawed ways of thinking that you are aware of in our culture today?

3. How might Satan used books, comedy, music, movies, and theater to sow the world into the hearts of people?

4. Why do you think the antichrists (deceivers) deny that Jesus is the Christ? Is this still Satan's modus operandi?

5. How do we allow the word of God to abide in us?

6. In 2:26, John uses the word "seduce" to describe what the antichrists seek to do to Christians. How is this different (if at all) from someone who teaches a false doctrine but sincerely believes it to be true?

Chapter 7

Fellowship and Righteousness

1 John 2:28-3:10

Life is serious business. How we live our Christian lives has consequences now and in the future. In the now, our choices can cause us to lose fellowship with God, which makes us easy marks for the allures of the world and the lies of the deceivers. Christians out of fellowship may walk in darkness and their day-to-day experience won't differ much from non-Christians. The New Testament points to an array of potential consequences for continuing rebelliousness including hindered prayer, loss of blessings, loss of the fruit of the Spirit, loss of peace, temporal discipline, an incapacity for deeper truths of the Word, and even physical death. In addition, there is the sobering reality that we will all stand before Jesus and give an account at the bema judgment. This has nothing to do with our destiny, eternal life, or status as God's children. This mortal life is a training program for the world to come. We are expected to learn and grow and be transformed as we walk in the Spirit and enjoy fellowship with our Creator. This faithfulness will result in commendation and other rewards when we stand before Jesus and give account, but it is possible for a Christian to stand before Jesus with little to show for the time they were given. In the imagery of First Corinthians 3, when a person's life is tested by fire, it is possible that all they have to show for it is smoke and ashes, the sad reality of opportunities squandered. It is possible to lose our reward, that is, to lose all of the commendation and other rewards that would have been ours had we lived faithfully. Every Christian should desire to live in fellowship with the Father and the Son, and that life enjoys confidence now and at the bema. That is the Christian life that will not result in shame at the bema.

Outline

V. THE PRACTICAL OUTWORKING OF LIVING IN FELLOWSHIP WITH GOD (2:28- 4:18)

   a. Abiding in God will result in confidence at the bema judgment (2:28)

   b. God's children are made visible by their God-righteousness as they abide in God, and the devil's children are made visible by their lack of God-righteousness (2:29-3:10)

      i. God is righteous and those that manifest His righteousness are His children (2:29)

      ii. We are blessed to be God's children, and our sure hope that purifies us is that when Jesus returns, we will be like him (3:1-3)

      iii. All sin is wickedness (3:4)

iv. The sinless Jesus died to take away sins (3:5)

v. Those abiding in fellowship with Jesus don't sin, but the one who sins has not seen or known him (3:5-6)

vi. The one who does God-righteousness is righteous, but the one who sins is of the devil (3:7-8)

vii. God's children don't sin and can't sin because His seed abides in them (3:9)

viii. God's children and the devil's children are made obvious by whether they exhibit God-righteousness, or fail to do so (3:10)

Scripture and Comments

John affirmed in the first chapter of his epistle that Christians sin. This forecloses any concept of sinless perfection during our mortal lifetime, but does it mean that Christians sin all the time? Some preachers relish describing how sinful Christians are. They repeatedly state that Christians are sinners and how Christians sin every day and maybe every hour. But is this true? While Christians certainly sin, is "sinners" an apt description of all Christians all the time? Are we always sinners in the hands of an angry God? Might we possibly be children in the warm embrace of a loving God? John brought needed balance and explained that the children of God are capable of living righteously and thereby manifesting themselves as God's children in a fallen world. They do this when they abide in fellowship with God.

1 John 2:28 And now, little children, abide in him; that, when he shall appear, we may have confidence, and not be ashamed before him at his coming.

This verse begins the longest unit within the epistle, a lengthy inclusio (2:28-4:21) that begins and ends with the theme of confidence and boldness at the bema. To this point, John informed his readers of his primary purpose of writing to them about fellowship with the Father and the Son (1:1-4), identified the central theological principle (1:5) that circumscribes any claims to fellowship with God, provided principles for experiencing such fellowship (1:6-2:11), confirmed and encouraged his readers as believers who had overcome the devil (2:12-14), and warned his readers about the dangers of the world system and the deceivers who deny that Jesus is the Christ (2:15-27). Although the preceding materials were not without exhortation, this verse launched the main body of the epistle because at this point John's focus turned to the central exhortation to **abide in** or remain in fellowship with the Father and the Son. He framed the exhortation within the theological concept of confidence and boldness at the bema. In what followed – between the bema judgment bookends of the inclusio – John argued that (1) believers are manifested as children of God by doing righteousness, which happens when we abide in fellowship (2:29-3:10), (2) righteousness is expressed and experienced with love as we abide (3:11-24), (3) believers must distinguish between the Spirit of God and the spirits of false prophets bent on deceiving us (4:1-6), and (4) believers must know and recognize God through love (4:7-16). The units of thought flow together and return us back in 4:17-18 to the issue of boldness and confidence at the bema judgment.

John's words **and now, little children** signaled the new unit of thought. Once again, his readers were his **little children** (teknion), the term Jesus used when he addressed the eleven (John 13:33). This was a term of affection and confirmation as fellow believers from the apostle to those he considered his spiritual offspring as a result of his ministry. The apostle Paul used this term of his readers in his letter to the Galatians (4:19) and John used it in First John 2:1, 2:12-13, 2:18, 3:7, 3:18, 4:4, and 5:21. John exhorted his readers to **abide in him**. The verb **abide** is the now familiar μένω (menō) that means to continue or remain in a place. We previously read this word in 2:6 ("abideth in him"), 2:10 ("abideth in the light), 2:14 ("abideth in you"), 2:17 ("abideth forever"), 2:19 ("continued with us"), and 2:24 ("abideth in you...remain in you...continue in the Son, and in the Father"). The directive to **abide in him** means to continue or remain in fellowship with **him**.

If they **abide in** fellowship with Jesus, then when **he** (Jesus) **shall appear,** they **may have confidence, and not be ashamed before him at his coming**. With these words, John linked present and future. Those who teach true grace – that sinners are justified by faith alone without works on the front end, a slate of promises or commitments or turning from sin at the moment of faith, or payment plans on the back end – are frequently criticized for giving people a license to sin. It is evident from Paul's writings that grace bandits were as abundant in the first century as today since they accused Paul of the same. True grace, however, provides no license, but the sobering reality that how we live really matters, yet it does not qualify or disqualify us as the children of God.

The reality is that in the future Jesus **shall appear**. The word **appear** translates the Greek φανερόω (phaneroō) and means "to cause to become visible, *reveal, expose publicly.*"[114] John earlier used this term in relation to the incarnation (1:2) and the antichrists (2:19), and in those instances it was translated "manifest" or "manifested." The word was used of Jesus' post-resurrection appearances to his disciples. (Mark 16:12, 14; John 21:1, 14) We are going to see Jesus and stand **before him at his coming**. The word **coming** is the Greek παρουσία (parousia) and means "arrival as the first stage in presence, *coming, advent.*"[115] The New Testament frequently uses this term in reference to the Lord's return. (e.g., Matthew 24:27, 37, 39; 1 Corinthians 15:23; 1 Thessalonians 2:19, 3:13, 4:15, 5:23; James 5:7) At this meeting at the return of our Lord, how we have lived will determine whether **we may have confidence...before him**, or instead **be ashamed before him**. John told his readers that those who **abide in** fellowship with Jesus now, will have **confidence...before him at his coming**. Implicitly, those who do not **abide in** fellowship with Jesus now will be **ashamed before him at his coming**. This is John's only use of the word **ashamed** in any of his writings, but it simply means to experience shame or disgrace. In Second John 8, John exhorted his readers: "Look to yourselves, that we lose not those things which we have wrought, but that we receive a full reward." Abiding in Jesus leads to **confidence...before him** and a full reward. We should all want that.

Before leaving this key verse, I want to briefly address some related words. The apostle Paul wrote: "For we must all appear before the judgment seat of Christ; that every one may receive the things *done* in *his* body, according to that

---

[114] William Arndt et al., *A Greek-English Lexicon of the New Testament*, 1048.
[115] Ibid., 780.

he hath done, whether *it be* good or bad." (2 Corinthians 5:10) He similarly wrote, "So then every one of us shall give account of himself to God." (Romans 14:12) These verses addressed exactly the same issue John did in First John 2:28 and Second John 8, namely that Christians will stand before Jesus Christ and give an account, and at that moment may be confident or ashamed of how they lived. What is at issue is not a weighing in the balances of our good and bad works to see whether the good outweighs the bad and we get into heaven. The question of our eternal destiny was settled at the moment we placed faith in Christ, and as we have already seen, John affirmed his readers had eternal life. The issue is living a life of faithfulness that pleases Jesus, with the result that we receive a commendation and reward. Some people struggle with this because they take the word "judgment" in a negative or punitive sense, but a judgment is simply a determination and has no inherent notion of punishment. The word "judgment seat" in 2 Corinthians 5:10 is the Greek noun βῆμα (bēma) and based on that, the doctrine is often referred to as the bema, bema seat, or bema judgment. In Corinth, there was an elevated bema seat in the town square where officials could sit and make pronouncements or render judgments, but in the future, it will be the Son of God appraising our faithfulness with a view to approval as the jeweler with a trained eye appraises the quality of a diamond. As God's children, we are all diamonds, but our faithfulness produces the valuable cuts, color, and clarity Jesus will appraise. It is no exaggeration that the doctrine of rewards is pervasive in the New Testament in the sense that nearly every writer makes at least some reference to it. As we are going to see, this doctrine is the theological anchor for the longest unit of material in First John.

> **1 John 2:29** If ye know that he is righteous,
> ye know that every one that doeth
> righteousness is born of him.

The subunit that continues through 3:10 links (1) the exhortation in 2:28 to abide and (2) the principle that we manifest ourselves as God's children by doing righteousness. It is the concept of abiding in (experiencing fellowship with) Jesus that produces righteousness and manifests or openly reveals us as children of God. Let me be absolutely clear on this point – we are not to push this principle beyond is moorings or flip it around. John never wrote that we are to determine if we are genuine Christians, or whether someone else is a genuine Christian, based on our perception of the presence of righteousness or good works. John never wrote that a person who does not reveal righteousness is not a genuine Christian.

John wrote that **if** you **know that he is righteous**. The balance of the verse makes clear that the pronoun **he** refers to God. Thus, **if** you **know that** God **is righteous**, you **know that every one that doeth righteousness is born of him**. John's use of **if** is not a first-class condition where the "if" is the equivalent of "since" and so assumes the truth of what followed, but neither does this mean John's readers did not **know that** God **is righteous**. As Hodges comments: "In the light of all that has been said by the apostle about these readers, it could have been assumed that they *did* know this. It is more likely that the conditional element is introduced because the readership was well aware that there were those who denied this truth about the nature of God."[116]

---

[116] Zane Clark Hodges, *The Epistle of John*, 126.

The word **just** translates the Greek adjective δίκαιος (dikaios) and is often translated as "righteous" (e.g., Romans 3:10, 5:7) and is usually so translated in First John (e.g., 2:1, 29; 3:7, 12). The related noun **righteousness** is the Greek δικαιοσύνη (dikaiosynē) and in this context means "the quality or characteristic of upright behavior, *uprightness, righteousness*."[117] Critically then, John related God's **righteousness** to the **righteousness** those **born of him** are capable of. This is not mere human or relative goodness that anyone is capable of. Rather, only those **born of him** can do this, and it is a visible manifestation that they are a child of God. For clarity, I will refer to this as "God-righteousness" in the remaining notes.

> **1 John 3:1** Behold, what manner of love the Father hath bestowed upon us, that we should be called the sons of God: therefore the world knoweth us not, because it knew him not. **2** Beloved, now are we the sons of God, and it doth not yet appear what we shall be: but we know that, when he shall appear, we shall be like him; for we shall see him as he is. **3** And every man that hath this hope in him purifieth himself, even as he is pure.

Building on the reference in the prior verse to being "born of him" and exhibiting God-righteousness, John told his readers to **behold** or understand **what manner of love the Father hath bestowed upon us, that we should be called the sons** or children **of God.** Here, agape **love**, the **love** of choice and volition, is in view. The reason the **world knoweth us** (the children **of God**) **not** is **because** the world did not know Jesus. As I addressed in the notes on First

---

[117] William Arndt et al., *A Greek-English Lexicon of the New Testament*, 248.

133

John 2:3, in this context "know" means an intimate and experiential knowledge of someone. Those who are a part of the **world** system may know historical facts about Jesus, but they lack an intimate and experiential knowledge of **him**. Likewise, as God's children we have a new nature within us that John explained in what followed as the source of our capacity to exhibit God-righteousness. When the child **of God** exhibits God-righteousness (see notes on 2:29), those who are a part of the **world** system do not have an intimate and experiential knowledge of the child **of God**. Even if they have some kind of relationship, they do not know the child **of God** with the understanding that comes with a more intimate knowledge because of this new nature within us that is entirely foreign to them and their experience of life.

John next addressed his readers as **beloved**, a term of intimacy, because while the **world** may not know his readers, he did. The word **beloved** translates the adjective ἀγαπητός (agapetos) and means "one who is in a very special relationship with another."[118] The word indicates that John considered his readers not only his "little children" but his good friends. John contrasted the present reality of being God's children with the future reality. **Now** or at the time John wrote, he and his readers were in fact **the sons** (or children) **of God**, and while they could exhibit God-righteousness they physically looked like everyone else. The future would bring a permanent transformation. Thus John added, **it doth** or does **not yet appear what we shall be** in the future. What we can **know** about the future for the child **of God** is **that, when he** (Jesus) **shall appear, we shall be like him**. As Hodges

---

[118] Ibid., 7.

observes: "Just as doing righteousness makes manifest a likeness to the righteous One, so also our future destiny involves the same principle: manifest likeness to Christ physically as well as spiritually."[119] God's children will enjoy resurrection bodies in the likeness of Jesus **when he shall appear**. From other passages we may reason that this will occur at the time of the "rapture" or gathering up (e.g., 1 Corinthians 15:51-57), but John did not elucidate further. Recall that the Greek term translated **appear** is the same Greek word translated as **appear** in 2:28 and is no doubt referencing the same event. The term was translated "manifest" or "manifested" in its earlier usages in 1:2 and 2:19.

It is unfortunate that for a variety of reasons, many Christians and church leaders have elected to downplay or outright ignore prophetic matters. They view these issues as divisive or without practical application. Yet this is exactly the opposite of the importance placed on prophetic matters in the Bible, which always views them as practical and life transforming. Here, John added in reference to our future resurrection that **every man that hath this hope in him** or in Jesus **purifieth himself, even as he** (Jesus) **is pure**. In the New Testament, the word **hope** almost always has a future orientation to it, as it does here. The word does not mean hopeful in the way that we **hope** our favorite team wins or our candidate gets elected. Rather, **this hope** is a firm conviction in the certainty of God's Word about something future, and in this instance, the resurrection.

The verb translated **purifieth** is the Greek ἁγνίζω (hagnizō) and means in this context "to cause to be morally

---

[119] Zane Clark Hodges, *The Epistle of John*, 129.

pure."[120] Having the sure and confident **hope in** Jesus concerning our future resurrection and entire likeness to **him** brings an experience of moral purity in the same way that Jesus is pure and holy. This is a strong statement with implications that John made explicit in 3:9. John *did not* qualify his statement – a person with **this hope in** Jesus will be *relatively* pure. Rather, it is Jesus' absolute and complete purity / holiness that is possible, but how can we possibly experience this quality of purity if we still sin? It is because we are presently **the sons of God.** We have been "born of him" (2:29) and while we are not yet fully transformed into the likeness of Jesus spiritually and physically, there is already within us something of the nature of God that makes it possible for us to exhibit God-righteousness (2:29). That "something" will be referred to as God's seed (3:9) and indicates that we already have a purified and sinless nature that is a part of who we are. This does not negate that part of us remains unredeemed – what the apostle Paul called the flesh. We have both at the same time, but are capable of living out the purified nature.

> **1 John 3:4** Whosoever committeth sin transgresseth also the law: for sin is the transgression of the law. **5** And ye know that he was manifested to take away our sins; and in him is no sin. **6** Whosoever abideth in him sinneth not: whosoever sinneth hath not seen him, neither known him.

In contrast to the purification in the prior verse, the person that **committeth sin transgresseth also the law.** This phrase implicates some translation issues that must be

---

[120] William Arndt et al., *A Greek-English Lexicon of the New Testament*, 12.

addressed. What is missed to the English reader is that the present tense verbs **committeth** and **transgresseth** are the same word in Greek. In the KJV, these words translate the Greek verb ποιέω (poieō), which can mean to make or manufacture something, but in this context simply means "to undertake or do something that brings about an event, state, or condition, *do, cause, bring about, accomplish, prepare,* etc."[121] Unfortunately, many modern translations add the words "practice" or "practices" or "makes a practice" in several places in 3:4-10. The ESV, for instance, translates the Greek verb poieō as "makes a practice" in 3:4, 8, and 9, as "practices" in 3:4 and 7, and as "practice" in 3:10. The CSB translates the second occurrence of the verb in 3:4 as "practices." Relatedly, some modern translations add something like "continues to" or "keeps on" before the word **sin** in 3:6 (e.g., ESV, NIV). These insertions reflect a theological commitment to make it easier to reconcile what John wrote in 3:4-10 with his statements in First John 1 that everyone has **sin** and sins.

The tests for life view of First John struggles with 3:4-10, tripping over the apostle's words about people who **sinneth not** (3:6), "he that doeth righteousness is righteous" (3:7), he "that committeth sin is of the devil" (3:8), and that those "born of God doth not commit sin" (3:9). So for example, instead of saying in 3:6 that **whosever abideth in him sinneth not** (KJV), the ESV emends the text to read, "no one who abides in him keeps on sinning." Advocates of the tests for life view acknowledge they sin, which means they fail the test in 3:6 as stated in the KJV with their understanding that abiding in Jesus is the equivalent of being a genuine believer. So they emend the

---

[121] Ibid., 839.

test so they can pass – one can "abide" in Christ and sin so long as they don't "keep[] on sinning." This alteration is theologically absurd, however, because God is light and in Him is no darkness at all (1:5). John meant exactly what he wrote – those who abide in Christ don't sin! Verse 7 presents a similar problem. The KJV reads, "he that doeth righteousness is righteous," but the ESV reads "practices righteousness is righteous." The ESV makes God grade the test on a curve – "practices" is squishy and means something like the test taker passes if he or she is usually but not always righteous. In any event, similar changes are made throughout the passage to prop up the tests for life view. I will not belabor this matter much further at this point except to emphasize that we cannot have it both ways. Either God is holy or God grades on a curve, but both of those propositions cannot be true.

Returning to the phrase **committeth sin transgresseth also the law**, the next translation challenge is the word **law**, which translates the Greek noun ἀνομία (anomia). The primary meaning is "state or condition of being disposed to what is lawless, *lawlessness.*"[122] Where the confusion comes in is that some readers understand the phrase to mean that **whosoever committeth sin transgresseth also the** Law of Moses (or the Old Testament law) even though nothing in the context supports this. Modern translations typically use "lawlessness" (i.e., "practices lawlessness" (ESV)), but even then many readers import the Law of Moses into the text. A better translation would simply be "iniquity" or "wickedness," and in fact the KJV frequently translates anomia as "iniquity" (e.g., Matthew 7:23, 13:41, 23:28, 24:12; Romans 4:7, 6:19). As Hodges explains:

[122] Ibid., 85.

The usage of the word *anomia* in biblical Greek (both in the New Testament and the Greek Old Testament) argues strongly that normally no such specific meaning as **lawlessness** was attached to this word. In the Septuagint translation of the Old Testament, we find *anomia* used to translate no less than twenty-four different Hebrew words. The most frequent one is the Hebrew *'awon*, for which English words like "wickedness," or "iniquity," are good equivalents. We should thus prefer the translation of this verse by the Confraternity Version (imprim. 1961): "Everyone who commits sin, commits iniquity also; and sin is iniquity." The apostle's statement is intended to stigmatize sin as "evil," "wicked," "iniquitous."[123]

With these translation matters in mind, 3:4 is not a hard verse to interpret. The person who engages in sin does iniquity or wickedness. Quite likely John had the deceivers in view, who were most probably engaging in sinful behavior while denying that their conduct was wicked. We see this in our modern culture and it is getting worse. Good is called evil, and evil good, but John was emphatic that **sin is the transgression of the law**, i.e., **sin is** wickedness. Bearing in mind the central theological predicate for the epistle – God is light and in Him is no darkness at all (1:5) – John's emphatic statement had practical implications.

Specifically, John's readers **know that** Jesus **was manifested to take away our sins; and in him is no sin.**

---

[123] Zane Clark Hodges, *The Epistle of John*, 132.

The student of John's Gospel will no doubt see in 3:6 the words from John 1:29: "The next day John seeth Jesus coming unto him, and saith, Behold the Lamb of God, which taketh away the sin of the world." A life of sin is the very opposite of the person (Jesus is sinless) and work (he died for our sins) of Jesus Christ. Sin is a serious matter for those who care about fellowship with a holy God. Indeed, **whosoever abideth in him sinneth not.** Here, John presented remarkably simple logic – the person who **abideth in** or is in fellowship with the sinless Jesus Christ will not sin so long as he or she continues to abide. We dare not alter the language to say the abiding believer won't sin much or won't keep on sinning. John's point is that the believer can enjoy fellowship with the Father and the Son, and this experience is a sinless one.

The negative side of John's conclusion is that **whosever sinneth hath not seen him, neither known him.** Again, it is not whoever "keeps on sinning" (ESV), but simply whoever sins **hath not seen him.** The verb **seen** is the Greek verb ὁράω (horaō) and can mean seeing with our eyes, but also can mean "to experience a condition or event"[124] or "to be mentally or spiritually perceptive, *perceive.*"[125] What is in view here is obviously not physical sight of Jesus with the eyes, but rather, seeing with the comprehension and perception of one in intimate fellowship with Jesus. We have a great example of this in Job 42:5: "I have heard of thee by the hearing of the ear: but now mine eye seeth thee." This is why John followed **hath not seen him** with **neither known him.** As addressed in the notes on the word "know" in First John 2:3, John used the word to indicate

124 William Arndt et al., *A Greek-English Lexicon of the New Testament*, 719.
125 Ibid., 720.

intimate knowledge and understanding as when Jesus rebuked Philip: "Jesus saith unto him, Have I been so long time with you, and yet hast thou not known me, Philip? he that hath seen me hath seen the Father; and how sayest thou *then*, Shew us the Father?" (John 14:9) Consistent with prior similar statements, John used the perfect tense for **seen** and **known**, denoting completed past actions with continuing consequences. John did not speak to what **whosoever** is capable of doing, but of what they were not presently experiencing.

Accordingly, the believer who abides in Jesus does not sin while he or she remains in fellowship with the sinless Son of God. The believer who commits a sin shows that at that moment he or she is not abiding in fellowship with the sinless Son of God and therefore has not **seen** or **known** Jesus in the sense of intimate fellowship and perception from a past point in time through the present. What is lost when we sin is continued fellowship, not our relationship to the Son, and when this happens, we have a means of regaining that intimate fellowship through confession and the receipt of forgiveness and restoration. (1 John 1:9)

> **1 John 3:7** Little children, let no man deceive you: he that doeth righteousness is righteous, even as he is righteous. **8** He that committeth sin is of the devil; for the devil sinneth from the beginning. For this purpose the Son of God was manifested, that he might destroy the works of the devil.

Here, John returned to his now familiar term of endearment **little children**. (1 John 2:1, 12, 28) In light of the preceding material in 2:29-3:6, his **little children** were to **let no man deceive** them concerning genuine or God-righteousness, which is entirely free of sin. John distinguished as mutually exclusive the two spheres concerning the nature of God and the nature of the **devil.** The person **that doeth righteousness is righteous, even as he is righteous.** This is nearly the same as what John stated in 2:29 where he explained that anyone who does the same quality of **righteousness** as that which characterizes God "is born of him." To distinguish relative good deeds that anyone is capable of, in the notes on 2:29 I referred to this as God-righteousness. John affirmed that the person who exhibited God-righteousness is in fact **righteous** just **as** God **is righteous.** This, of course, raises questions for us because we know, and because John affirmed in the first chapter of his epistle, that Christians still sin, but the point here is that Christians are capable of God-righteousness. The enabling capacity for God-righteousness is explained in 3:9, namely that God's "seed remaineth in him."

While God is **righteous** and Christians can live out God-righteousness, they can also sin, and when they do so they follow the example of the **devil.** John explained that the person **that committeth sin is of the devil; for the devil sinneth from the beginning.** Since everyone sins, as John confirmed in the first chapter of his epistle and we know from experience, the phrase **of the devil** does not mean unsaved or else we must accept that everyone is lost. In reality, everyone is capable of being **of the devil** when they follow his example. The **devil sinneth from the beginning,** which likely means from his first appearance in the Garden in Genesis 3. No doubt he sinned before that moment, but from the vantage point of the reader of the Bible, Satan is first encountered in Genesis 3 trying to deceive Eve. The verb **sinneth** is present tense and here is used to confirm that Satan sinned from the beginning and is still does. When a person exhibits God-righteousness he or she manifests God (who **is righteous**), but when a person sins, they reflect or follow the devil's example and do his bidding. When the apostle Peter rebuked Jesus, he was sternly reprimanded: "Get thee behind me, Satan...for thou savourest not the things that be of God, but those that be of men." (Matthew 16:23)

Recall the central principle that God is light and in him is no darkness at all. When we do God-righteousness, that is of God, meaning it is sourced in Him and reflects His nature and example. Likewise, to sin is to act like the **devil** and such behavior is sourced in him. The deceivers likely wanted to make a claim to **righteousness** while acting like the **devil**. John's readers were to exercise discernment and not be deceived by such absurdities. Indeed, John's readers needed to understand how antithetical to the purpose and work of Jesus Christ it would be for one to claim **righteousness** while acting like the **devil**. John explained that the **purpose** or goal of the incarnation – that **the Son of God was manifested** – was to **destroy the works of the devil**. Jesus took away our sins and inaugurated the New Covenant that will culminate in the complete eradication of all vestiges of sin and the **devil**. To act in a way that is sourced in the **devil** and reflects his nature and example is to do the very thing Jesus' incarnation purposed to put an end to. We will see later that the deceivers denied the incarnation, and so it is not surprising that they would live antithetically to the primary purposes of the incarnation.

> **1 John 3:9** Whosoever is born of God doth not commit sin; for his seed remaineth in

> him: and he cannot sin, because he is born
> of God. 10 In this the children of God are
> manifest, and the children of the devil:
> whosoever doeth not righteousness is not of
> God, neither he that loveth not his brother.

Here we find what is probably the most debated portion of the epistle. The person **born of God doth not commit sin** because God's **seed remaineth in him: and he cannot sin, because he is born of God**. As I referenced earlier, many modern translations emend the text in a misguided attempt to align the difficult verses John included in First John 3, the tests for life theory, and the reality that all Christians sin. For instance, the ESV reads, "No one born of God makes a practice of sinning," but that is not what John intended. Where John wrote in absolutes, modern translations manufacture a gray area that creates more problems than they solve. It is not just that Christians sin, but also that they never stop doing so. Indeed, we may rightly say that all Christians continue to sin or make a practice of sinning until they die. So while the modern translations attempt to separate genuine Christians from those that practice sin, the reality is that all genuine Christians practice sin. The emendation accomplishes nothing and is not supported by the Greek text. As Hodges comments, had John wanted to express the idea of continuing in sin he could have done so much more clearly than simply using a present tense verb:

> There is no doubt that in an appropriate
> context the Greek present tense can have a
> present progressive force like "he is
> sinning." But the introduction of ideas like
> "continue to" or "to go on doing" require

more than the Greek tense to make them intelligible. For this purpose there were Greek words available which are actually used in the New Testament. For example, *diapantos* occurs in Luke 24:53: "... and [they] were *continually* in the temple praising and blessing God." The same word occurs in Hebrews 13:15: "Therefore by Him let us *continually* offer the sacrifice of praise to God." (See also: Mark 5:5; Acts 10:2; 24:16; Romans 11:10; Hebrews 9:6). The Greek phrase *eis to diēnekes* could have the same meaning (cf. Hebrews 7:3; 10:1). The Greek present tense did not by itself convey such ideas....[126]

John's reference to the person **born of God** unquestionably pointed to a believer. He wrote in the Fourth Gospel: "But as many as received him, to them gave he power to become the sons of God, even to them that believe in his name. Which were born, not of blood, nor of the will of the flesh, nor of the will of man, but of God." (John 1:12-13) John unequivocally stated that because God's **seed remaineth in** the person **born of God**, he or she **doth not commit sin**. The interpretive key lays in the word **seed**. The Greek noun σπέρμα (sperma) means "the source from which something is propagated, *seed*."[127] The idea then is that in some way **God** is propagated within the believer. As God is spirit (John 4:24), His **seed** should be understood as spiritual in nature. As **God** is light, holy, and sinless, so also is His

[126] Zane Clark Hodges, *The Epistle of John*, 143.
[127] William Arndt et al., *A Greek-English Lexicon of the New Testament*, 937.

seed. The **seed** then places the very nature of God within the immaterial aspect of the believer, and that part of the believer **doth not commit sin**. Peter similarly wrote: "Being born again, not of corruptible seed, but of incorruptible, by the word of God, which liveth and abideth for ever." (1 Peter 1:23) As believers we have this new nature and at the same time part of us is not yet fully redeemed, which Paul referred to as the flesh. We have the ability, when we abide in fellowship with God and so yield control to this new nature, to exhibit God-righteousness that is wholly without **sin**.

John continued, explaining that **in this the children of God are manifest, and the children of the devil**. The issue here is not whether we are in fact **children of God**, but whether we **are manifest** or visibly revealed in our actions as such. The word **manifest** is the Greek adjective φανερός (phaneros) and has the primary meaning of "being evident so as to be readily known, *visible, clear, plainly to be seen, open, plain, evident, known.*"[128] Recall where this unit started with the idea of boldness and confidence when we stand before Jesus Christ, and with the observation that we are rightly "called the sons of God." (1 John 2:28-3:1) The key to the confidence and boldness at that future time is abiding in fellowship with God now. When we do that, it is the redeemed and sinless part of us, God's **seed**, that is in the driver's seat. This results in actual God-righteousness so that we openly and visibly reflect our true identify as **children of God**. When we don't do that – when we don't abide in fellowship with God and live from our new nature but instead sin – we take on the visible appearance of **children**

of the devil as we openly do his works. In this sense, to be a child of God or the devil is to reflect their nature, and Christians who still have the flesh to contend with can act like the devil with a straight face.

The next statement bridged the subunit that began in 2:28 and ended in 3:10 with the material concerning love that followed. The prior statement about manifesting as a child **of God** or **of the devil** can be focused in on the command to love one another. Thus, John wrote that the person that **doeth not righteousness is not of God, neither he that loveth not his brother** or fellow believer. The person that does not do God-righteousness does not visibly reflect the nature and example **of God**. And more specifically, the person that **loveth not his brother** does not visibly reflect the nature and example **of God**. By implication, this failure reflects the nature and example of the **devil**. The way in which our love or lack thereof reflects the nature of God or the devil naturally leads into a more focused discussion of the role of love in the abiding life.

Closing

It is unfortunate that the profound doctrinal statements John shared with his readers in 2:28-3:10 have too often been lost in the shuffle primarily due to the tests for salvation metric that has been forced upon First John. When we let the text speak for itself, it does so with John's usual impeccable logic. John brought balance to the discussion of Christians and sin. We can acknowledge the reality that Christians sin with the reality that as children of God we share in the divine nature and therefore have the capacity to live righteously as we walk in fellowship with God. This new nature that results from God's seed remaining in us allows us to make God's righteousness and love visible in a dark world, to be a beacon of light. On the other hand, with our old nature we remain quite capable of reflecting the devil and his hate. The decision to walk in fellowship would be better described as a commitment. It is not one we make to become a Christian, but one every Christian should eagerly embrace anew every day of their lives. We should want fellowship with our Creator. We should want to reflect His righteousness. We should want to please Him and have confidence at the bema.

Application Points

- MAIN PRINCIPLE: Living in fellowship with God follows the lead of our new nature sourced in His seed that remains in us, and this sinless experience manifests God-righteousness, but Christians out of fellowship fall back on the old nature and manifest the example of the devil.

- Living in fellowship with God will result in confidence at the bema.

Discussion Questions

1. What are some passages outside of First John that reference the bema judgment or rewards or inheritance for believers?

2. What are the rewards available to believers at the bema judgment?

3. Do you believe that you walk in fellowship with God routinely or rarely?

4. What are the biggest challenges you struggle with regarding fellowship with God?

5. What is the difference between good works that anyone can do and exhibit God-righteousness?

6. How is hope in the New Testament different from being hopeful?

Chapter 8

Fellowship and Love
1 John 3:11-18

In the prior chapter we saw that because God's children have His seed abiding in them, they are capable of manifesting God-righteousness in a way that visibly identifies them as children of God. Not only does the world not know God's children, it hates them when they live out God's righteousness. We see it in the lives of Cain and Abel and we see it today as Christians are increasingly marginalized and persecuted when they live out God's righteousness. However the world may defend its actions, we know the issue is one of light and darkness. We know those in the darkness hate the light because their deeds are evil. When we live righteously, we shine a light in a dark world that is offensive to many. Even though there are many like Cain who despise righteousness in others, some may see our testimony and begin to seek God. Of all things, it is most important that they see a quality of love among us that is unparalleled and never duplicated in the world system. It is within the fundamental needs of every human being to experience that quality of love. We live in a culture that traffics in the language of love but not the reality of love that Jesus displayed during his earthly ministry. The world's counterfeits go unchallenged if Christians fail to display the genuine article, and it is uniquely those in fellowship with God that put His love on display to the world.

Outline

V. THE PRACTICAL OUTWORKING OF LIVING IN FELLOWSHIP WITH GOD (2:28- 4:18)

    a. Abiding in God will result in confidence at the bema judgment (2:28)

    b. God's children are made visible by their God-righteousness as they abide in God, and the devil's children are made visible by their lack of God-righteousness (2:29-3:10)

    c. The world is hostile to righteousness (3:11-18)

        i. The command they heard from the beginning is to love one another (3:11)

        ii. Cain did not love his brother, but murdered him because his deeds were evil and his brother's righteous (3:12)

        iii. Do not be surprised if the world hates you for being righteous (3:13)

        iv. Love for the brethren confirms we have passed from death to life, but the one who hates a brother or sister abides in death (3:14-15)

        v. We understand love because Jesus died for us and showed us how we ought to love the brethren in action and truth (3:16-18)

Scripture and Comments

John's chief exhortation in First John 2:28-4:18 was to abide in fellowship with God. In the last chapter we saw how walking in fellowship with God manifests His righteousness and our true identity as His children. Now the focus of God-righteousness is sharpened to the prime directive that we love the brethren.

> **1 John 3:11** For this is the message that ye heard from the beginning, that we should love one another. **12** Not as Cain, *who* was of that wicked one, and slew his brother. And wherefore slew he him? Because his own works were evil, and his brother's righteous. **13** Marvel not, my brethren, if the world hate you.

The **message that** his readers **heard from the beginning** of their Christian walk was **that we should love one another.** He previously described this **message in** First John 2:7-11 as "an old commandment which ye had from the beginning...which ye have heard from the beginning" and a "new commandment." John stated that those who hate their brother are in darkness (2:11) but "he that loveth his brother abideth in the light" (2:10).

Cain was the prototypical negative example. He was **of that wicked one,** a clear reference to the devil (see 3:10), because he **slew his brother** Abel. This alludes to the familiar story found in Genesis 4, where the first murder occurred. **Cain** and Abel were two of the sons of Adam and Eve. In that passage, God "had respect unto Abel and his offering: but unto Cain and to his offering he had not respect." (Genesis 4:4-5) As a consequence of God's reaction to their respective offerings, "Cain was very wroth." Indeed, God told **Cain** that if he does not do well, "sin lieth at the door" and desires to control him. God's warning was not heeded, and "Cain rose up against Abel his brother, and slew him." (Genesis 4:8) With this in mind, John asked and answered the question of why **Cain** murdered Abel. Then John responded to his own question, **because his own works were evil, and his brother's righteous**. The envy and hate **Cain** exhibited toward Abel was grounded in Cain's wickedness. The wicked hate light and righteousness. (John 3:19-21) That principle remained true when John penned his epistle and remains true today. We should not push the illustration too far and insist that **Cain** was necessarily lost. The Bible never says that, and we know even a man after God's own heart (King David) could murder.

Applying the Old Testament illustration to his readers, John concluded, **Marvel not, my brethren**, or in other words do not be surprised, **if the world hate you**. The animosity **Cain** showed Abel illustrated how **the world** (the people in the **world** system and especially the deceivers or antichrists) would respond to believers who exhibit God-righteousness like Abel did. This creates the irony that the allegedly tolerant **world** that professes to accept everyone in fact hates those who display God-righteousness, including those who do so by loving their brothers and sisters in Christ. Yet they will readily embrace nearly any kind of unrighteousness and call it righteousness.

> **1 John 3:14** We know that we have passed from death unto life, because we love the brethren. He that loveth not *his* brother

abideth in death. **15** Whosoever hateth his brother is a murderer: and ye know that no murderer hath eternal life abiding in him.

John made the powerful statement that **we know that we have passed from death unto life**. Many readers will recognize this language from John 5:24: "Verily, verily, I say unto you, He that heareth my word, and believeth on him that sent me, hath everlasting life, and shall not come into condemnation; but is passed from death unto life." No doubt John had this in mind when he encouraged his readers about what they can **know**. This is not the verb ginoskō that John previously used (e.g., 2:3-5), but οἶδα (oida), which has a range of meaning from having information to "be[ing] intimately acquainted with or stand in a close relation to, *know*."[129] Hodges comments that the range of meaning includes "direct, immediate knowledge" or experiential knowledge.[130] As Christians, we **know** as an intellectual fact "that we have passed from death unto life" based on the veracity of God's promises in verse like John 3:16. We also **know** this experientially **because we love the brethren**. Many have twisted this verse into a "test for life" based on self-assessment of personal works rather than God's promises, but that was not even on John's radar.

Lived truth brings to us a different quality of knowledge, and here, that difference is grounded in relating the experience of loving **the brethren** (an outworking of God-righteousness) with experiencing **life**. The opposite also follows – unloving attitudes (**he that loveth not his brother**) bring an experience of abiding **in death**. The

---

[129] William Arndt et al., *A Greek-English Lexicon of the New Testament*, 693.
[130] Zane Clark Hodges, *The Epistle of John*, 157.

apostle Paul confirmed this in his famous verse that is often misunderstood as a justification verse rather than a sanctification verse: "For the wages of sin is death: but the gift of God is eternal life through Jesus Christ our Lord." We are justified by faith alone, but whether we experience abiding **in death** or **life** depends on our walk, and according to John, it comes down to love. The concept of abiding **in death** concerns quality of **life** just as the concept of eternal **life** is as much about quality as it is duration. Jesus promised abundant **life** (John 10:10) and that is in view here. The quality of **life** in fellowship with God is entirely different than it is without fellowship, and in fact the latter is so much worse that it is called **death**. This is not physical **death** but the sense of separation or distance that we experience when there is a rift in what was previously a close relationship. We are always God's children but when there is a rift resulting from a lack of love that experience is called **death**.

Not only does the unloving Christian **abideth in death** but like Cain the unloving Christian that **hateth his brother is a murderer**. Even without causing the physical death of another, harboring hate toward a brother is to harbor the same heart attitude Cain had toward Abel. Employing the verb oida, John explained that **we know that no murderer hath eternal life abiding in him**. The issue here is not whether someone is a genuine or spurious believer. That John puts his propositions in terms of fellow **brethren** places the focus on relationships among believers. The issue is not whether the murderous believer **hath eternal life** but whether he or she **hath eternal life abiding in him**. This matter of passing **from death unto life** is not empty words or ivory tower academics, but goes directly to our daily experience of **life** or **death**. When we are unloving it is not the victim of our hatred that suffers but us because we are not experiencing the fullness of **eternal life**. We experience the best possible quality of **life** when we have **eternal life abiding in** us, and that only happens when we are in fellowship with God and doing God-righteousness including loving the **brethren**. The question we must wrestle with is why we would ever choose to experience **death** instead of **life**.

> **1 John 3:16** Hereby perceive we the love *of God*, because he laid down his life for us: and we ought to lay down *our* lives for the brethren. **17** But whoso hath this world's good, and seeth his brother have need, and shutteth up his bowels *of compassion* from him, how dwelleth the love of God in him? **18** My little children, let us not love in word, neither in tongue; but in deed and in truth.

Having addressed the prototypical negative example of non-**love** in the life of Cain, John provided the prototypical positive example of **love** from the life of Jesus Christ. We **perceive** or understand **the love of God, because he laid down his life for us**. In the KJV, the words "of God" are in italics because they do not appear in the Greek text. Literally, it reads, "we have come to know love." The verb **perceive** (or know or understand) is in the perfect tense ("have come to know") indicating a past completed action with continuing consequences. The phrase **he laid down his life for us** necessarily means the work of Christ is in view. We have come to have a first-hand understanding of **love** because of Jesus's work at the cross, and he also provided us the prototypical example of perfect **love** so that **we ought to lay down our lives for the brethren.**

Of course, we may be called upon to give our physical **lives**, but the logical implication is that if the prototypical example of **love** is paying the ultimate price, then doing anything less should naturally flow from **love**. Accordingly, **whoso hath this world's good, and seeth his** Christian **brother have need, and shutteth up his bowels of compassion from him**, has failed to meet the standard. Having proposed this hypothetical, John answered with the rhetorical question, **how dwelleth the love of God in him?** The answer demanded is that this Christian does not have **the love of God** dwelling or abiding (Greek menō) **in him**. If **the love of God** is not abiding in us, this does not mean we are fake believers. It means we are out of fellowship and not experiencing eternal life abiding in us, but instead experiencing death (3:14-15).

John spoke plainly about our responsibility to our fellow believers again employing his favorite term of endearment, **my little children**. This term, of course, would never have been used to speak of fake or spurious believers. The application is simple: **let us not love in word, neither in tongue, but in deed and in truth**. His point was that **love requires more than** speech (**word**) or use of the **tongue**. Such **love** requires action in conformity with **truth**. Recall from chapter 1 that the word **truth** is the Greek ἀλήθεια (alētheia) and in John's writings conveys God's reality, the cornerstone of which is His nature and works including His redemptive work through Jesus Christ, the Christian model for **love** expressed in 3:16.

Closing

The secular culture gets love wrong, but it is notable how pervasive the concept of love is in our culture. It dominates our music, movies, literature, and thought life, and for good reason. We were created in the image of God. If it is true that God is love, as the Bible affirms, then we may infer that we were created to have the capacity to love as God loves. After the Fall, humanity still bears God's image, though tarnished. Humanity is still designed for genuine love, but that too is tarnished. Fallen humanity strives for love because they were designed for it, but because of the Fall the love they seek and achieve is often corrupt and at best is far less than the fullness of the love that God is. That's why the culture is obsessed with love, and even in love with the idea of love. It is also why the people of the world are empty. What they desperately need cannot be obtained from the world. The Christian can experience this love, and manifest it in this world, as they walk in fellowship with God. We should never take for granted the unique privilege we have to experience God in this way, or the unique opportunity we have to demonstrate love to those that need it most.

Application Points

- MAIN PRINCIPLE: The Christian that walks in fellowship with God has passed from death to life, and is aware of that transition as they love their brethren in deed and in truth following the example of Jesus, who laid down his life for us.

- When Christians manifest God-love the world will not comprehend them.

Discussion Questions

1. Why did Cain kill Abel?

2. Do you think Cain was a believer? Why or why not?

3. In practical terms, when John says we have passed from death unto life, what does that mean? What difference does it make in our daily lives?

4. Why is it the case that if a person hates his brother, he is a murderer?

5. How would you define eternal life?

6. Short of physically dying for someone else, how do we lay down our lives for our brothers and sisters in Christ?

7. What does it look like to love in word or tongue but not deed and truth?

Chapter 9

Fellowship and Prayer

1 John 3:19-24

The Old and New Testament consistently teach that how we live impacts our prayer life. For example, we read that "whoso stoppeth his ears at the cry of the poor, he also shall cry himself, but shall not be heard." (Proverbs 21:13) James wrote: "Ye ask, and receive not, because ye ask amiss, that ye may consume it upon your lusts." (James 4:3) Numerous other verses fortify this simple principle – those close to God have their prayers answered and those walking in darkness don't have their prayers answered. I don't mean by this that those close to God get whatever they put on their Christmas list. Rather, those close to God experience His holiness and His love and it changes their priorities and ultimately their prayer life. Their prayers line up with the character and will of God. What we will learn in this chapter is that those who walk in fellowship with God have confidence in prayer and their prayers are answered. At this point, we should not be surprised based on the benefits of fellowship we have already examined. Abiding in Him produces confidence in this life and in the life to come.

Outline

V. THE PRACTICAL OUTWORKING OF LIVING IN FELLOWSHIP WITH GOD (2:28- 4:18)

a. Abiding in God will result in confidence at the bema judgment (2:28)

b. God's children are made visible by their God-righteousness as they abide in God, and the devil's children are made visible by their lack of God-righteousness (2:29-3:10)

c. The world is hostile to righteousness (3:11-18)

d. Those who show God-love for the brethren experience confidence in prayer (3:19- 24)

   i. We know we belong to the truth and experience confidence in prayer because of our God-love for the brethren (3:19)

   ii. Even if we have doubts about our motives, we can have confidence that God knows all (3:20)

   iii. If we don't have doubts, we enjoy confidence in prayer and receive our requests because of our obedience (3:21-22)

   iv. God commands that we believe in the name of His Son, Jesus Christ and love one another (3:23)

   v. The one who obeys enjoys mutually abiding with God and knows from the Holy Spirit that God abides in him or her (3:24)

Scripture and Comments

Fellowship is the central ingredient for a confident prayer life. It is only in fellowship that we live out our new nature, and we should not be surprised that when our new nature is in the driver's seat, it radically impacts our prayer life. Our prayers no longer sound like wish lists but love lists as our priorities are reoriented toward the wellbeing of others and spiritual matters. In the passage that follows, John transitioned from the relationship between fellowship and love to the relationship between fellowship and prayer.

> **1 John 3:19** And hereby we know that we are of the truth, and shall assure our hearts before him. **20** For if our heart condemn us, God is greater than our heart, and knoweth all things.

Not only is doing works of love central to exhibiting God-righteousness (3:10b-18), but it provides confirmation that **we are of the truth**. To be **of the truth** is to be in conformity with **the truth**, and here John likely had in mind especially the model of love demonstrated in Jesus Christ's redemptive work. As a consequence of showing God-love for the brethren, John and his readers would also **assure** their **hearts before** God. The noun "heart" is the Greek work καρδία (kardia) and means the "seat of physical, spiritual and mental life."[131] The point then is to have an inner confidence or certainty of mind **before him** (God) in prayer (compare 3:22). John recognized the possibility that a believer might love others yet entertain doubts about the sufficiency or motives of their actions.

---

[131] William Arndt et al., *A Greek-English Lexicon of the New Testament*, 508.

Those doubts may or may not be well-founded. Our uncertainty about our own **hearts** must be counterbalanced by what we know of God. John therefore added that **if our heart condemn us, God is greater than our heart, and knoweth all things**. If we are loving others as we should yet harbor inward doubts, we can take solace in God's complete knowledge of the matter. At some point we have to stop the mental hand wringing and leave it in the hands of the only one qualified to sort it out. What we cannot do is let those doubts paralyze us in our walk. Instead, we must continue loving and praying.

> **1 John 3:21** Beloved, if our heart condemn us not, *then* have we confidence toward God. **22** And whatsoever we ask, we receive of him, because we keep his commandments, and do those things that are pleasing in his sight. **23** And this is his commandment, That we should believe on the name of his Son Jesus Christ, and love one another, as he gave us commandment.

John again referred to his readers as **beloved** (dear friends) as he did in 3:2. Having addressed the negative – where "our heart condemns us" with inward doubts – John next addressed the positive: **if our heart condemn us not, then have we confidence toward God** in prayer. The specific **confidence** is that **whatsoever we ask, we receive of him, because we keep his commandments, and do those things that are pleasing in his sight**. John's point was not that a believer always receives what he or she requests in prayer. Instead, this assurance was to those who **keep** God's **commandments, and do those things that are pleasing in his sight**. We need not guess which **commandments** John had in view because he specifically stated them: **That we should believe on the name of his Son Jesus Christ, and love one another, as he gave us commandment.** Any possible misunderstanding about the contours of this promise were resolved later in the epistle where John clarified that it is praying according to God's will that is in view: "[I]f we ask anything according to his will, he heareth us: and if we know that he hear us, whatsoever we ask, we know that we have the petitions that we desired of him." (1 John 5:14-15) The picture John painted was not that with enough faith we'd get whatever we want. Rather, it is obedience that results in **confidence toward God** in prayer and answered prayers. This obedience brings our hearts and actions in line with the will of God and transforms our prayer life so that **confidence** follows.

Note that the commandment that **we should believe on the name of his Son Jesus Christ** means to exercise faith in the person and works (i.e., the **name**) of God's **Son Jesus Christ**. It was this very point that the Gnostics that flourished in the second century would attack. They allowed that a human named Jesus was crucified, but not the **Son** of God. The deceivers apparently pressed a similar heresy, and John confirmed that our faith must rest in the finished work of **Jesus**, who is both the **Son** of God and the **Christ** or Messiah. A Christian that departs from that has no basis for **confidence** in prayer.

> **1 John 3:24** And he that keepeth his commandments dwelleth in him, and he in him. And hereby we know that he abideth in us, by the Spirit which he hath given us.

In the preceding verses, the apostle explained that obedience leads to confidence in prayer, but at this point he added another benefit of obedience. The believer **that keepeth his commandments dwelleth in him, and he in him**. The word **dwelleth** is the now familiar Greek verb menō that throughout First John is translated with similar terms such as abide, remain, or dwell. To this point, John referenced believers being **in him** (e.g., 2:5, 2:6, 2:27, 2:28, 3:6), but he had not yet explicitly mentioned the idea of God **in** us, though he confirmed that God's "seed remaineth in him." (1 John 3:9) Accordingly, John's statement that another benefit of obedience is God abiding or dwelling in us started a new subunit.

The concept that believers can abide in God while God abides in them was expressly taught by Jesus following the last supper: "Abide in me, and I in you. As the branch cannot bear fruit of itself, except it abide in the vine; no more can ye, except ye abide in me. I am the vine, ye *are* the branches: He that abideth in me, and I in him, the same bringeth forth much fruit: for without me ye can do nothing." (John 15:4-5) Jesus also explained that those who "hath my commandments, and keepeth them, he it is that loveth me: and he that loveth me shall be loved of my Father, and I will love him, and will manifest myself to him." (John 14:21) When asked how Jesus would manifest himself to the apostles, he responded: "If a man love me, he will keep my words: and my Father will love him, and we will come unto him, and make our abode with him." (John 14:23) The phrase "make our abode" or "make our home" is again the Greek verb menō, translated as **dwelleth** and as **abideth** in 3:24. Obedience to the **commandments** results in abiding / dwelling in God and God abiding / dwelling in us. In other words, obedience to the **commandments** produces fellowship, an intimacy grounded in a mutual sharing inherent in the experience of abiding.

After presenting this new concept of mutual abiding, John added that **hereby we know that** God **abideth in us, by the Spirit which he hath given us.** At this point, John did not explain exactly how **the Spirit** gives believers assurance that God **abideth in us,** but John would repeat his statement in 4:13 forming an inclusio marking off the next subunit. We should note that John previously addressed the ministry of the Holy **Spirit** but referred there to the "unction" (2:20) and the "anointing" (2:27). Now John saw fit to expressly identify the Holy **Spirit** to set the stage for addressing other spirits that bring false doctrine in the verses that follow.

<u>Closing</u>

Your mission, should you choose to accept it, is to identify and read the prayers of the apostle Paul in the New Testament. They include Romans 1:8-10, 10:1, 12:12, 15:5-6, 15:30-33; 1 Corinthians 1:4-9, 16:23; 2 Corinthians 1:3-7, 2:14-16, 9:12-15, 12:7-9, 13:7-9; Galatians 6:18; Ephesians 1:3 ff., 1:15-23, 3:14-21, 6:19-20; Philippians 1:3-6, 1:9-11, 4:6-7; Colossians 1:3-14, 4:2-4; 1 Thessalonians 1:2-3, 2:13-16, 3:9-13, 5:23-24; 2 Thessalonians 1:3 ff., 1:11-12, 2:16-17, 3:2-5, 3:16; 1 Timothy 1:12, 2:1 ff.; 2 Timothy 1:3-7, 4:22; Philemon 4-7, 25. Paul unquestionably walked in fellowship with God, and reading his prayers gives us insight into how believers in fellowship with God pray. You will find that Paul's prayers rarely focused on himself and usually focused on the spiritual well-being of others. Try to incorporate aspects of Paul's prayers into your prayer life as you pray for others. I recommend keeping a written prayer list and making a point to pray for specific individuals by name, even those that never asked you to and won't know you did. Pray for physical and financial needs, but most of all pray for their spiritual growth. Pray for your pastor or elders and your church. Pray for your personal ministry and sphere of influence. Pray with confidence and watch.

Application Points

- MAIN PRINCIPLE: Walking in fellowship with God results in confidence in prayer as our obedience reorients our priorities and concerns around the will of God.

- The fellowship available to the believer is "me in God and God in me."

Discussion Questions

1. What is the practical difference between praying with confidence and praying without confidence?

2. Do you ever experience self-doubt about your motives?

3. John added a critical nuance to his theology of fellowship when he stated that it is mutual, that is, us in God and God in us. How is this different than just us in God?

4. Does God grant prayers just because we strongly believe he will give us what we asked for?

5. Does God grant prayers when we don't believe He will grant them?

Chapter 10

Fellowship and Discernment
1 John 4:1-6

We live in a world saturated in secularism. A Hedonistic mindset and various philosophies from materialistic naturalism to Marxism prevail. Hate and indoctrination are the currency of the day under the branding of tolerance and fact checkers. Church history shows us that the world's ideas about everything, including religion, can easily become entrenched among Christians. Sometimes outsiders bring it in, and sometimes insiders show their true colors, as the antichrists in John's day had done. Unfortunately, Christians can be easy marks, but there is no excuse for naiveté or ignorance because we have been warned. Living in the last hour enjoins us to develop discernment. Jesus told his disciples as he sent them on mission to be shrewd "as serpents, and harmless as doves." (Matthew 10:16) To do this we have to know the truth-reality. It is imperative that we make the study of God's Word a routine life practice. We should know God's Book better than anything else. This requires diligence, time, and rigor. This requires the heart attitude of a

168

learner, who is ready to be wrong and even welcomes God's correction when it comes. Lots of Christians look at God's Word for confirmation and not transformation. The latter requires renewing the mind and that only happens as we discover we were wrong and welcome the truth. Adding to our challenges, the devil has had millennia to hone his skills in deception. A lethargic approach to the Scriptures won't be good enough. Fortunately, it is not just our own resources and self-discipline. We have the Holy Spirit and can learn to test what we hear and distinguish truth from lies.

<u>Outline</u>

V. THE PRACTICAL OUTWORKING OF LIVING IN FELLOWSHIP WITH GOD (2:28- 4:18)

    a. Abiding in God will result in confidence at the bema judgment (2:28)

    b. God's children are made visible by their God-righteousness as they abide in God, and the devil's children are made visible by their lack of God-righteousness (2:29-3:10)

    c. The world is hostile to righteousness (3:11-18)

    d. Those who show God-love for the brethren experience confidence in prayer (3:19- 24)

    e. Discern between the Spirit of Truth and Spirit of Error (4:1-6)

        i. Test the spirits to determine if they are from God (4:1)

ii. The Spirit that confesses that Jesus has come in the flesh is from God, but the spirit that does not so confess is the spirit of the antichrist (4:2-3)

iii. John's readers have overcome the deceivers, who are from the world and speak the world's words, and the world listens (4:4-5)

iv. The apostles are from God, and those that know God hear them and those not from God don't hear them (4:6)

Scripture and Comments

John returned to the subject that occasioned his writing of the epistle, namely the antichrists or deceivers who sought to seduce his readers. It was critical that they exercise discernment to distinguish truth from error.

> **1 John 4:1** Beloved, believe not every spirit, but try the spirits whether they are of God: because many false prophets are gone out into the world. **2** Hereby know ye the Spirit of God: Every spirit that confesseth that Jesus Christ is come in the flesh is of God: **3** And every spirit that confesseth not that Jesus Christ is come in the flesh is not of God: and this is that *spirit* of antichrist, whereof ye have heard that it should come; and even now already is it in the world.

Building on what he just wrote about abiding and the Holy Spirit, John's next subunit (4:1-4:6) urged his **beloved** readers to exercise discernment because of the deceivers.

John's exhortation was that they **believe not every spirit, but try the spirits whether they are of God**. The word **spirit** is the Greek noun πνεῦμα (pneuma) and can have a wide range of meanings. To get at John's intended meaning in this context, we are helped by his explanation of why his readers needed to test or **try** every **spirit**, namely that **many false prophets are gone out into the world**. John's obvious point was not to blindly accept everything they heard as truth, but to test what they heard. John was interested in the *source* of the teaching, whether it was **the Spirit of God** or some other **spirit**. Every person has an immaterial aspect of their person that can be referred to as his or her **spirit** (e.g., Romans 8:16; Hebrews 4:12) and is "the source and seat of insight, feeling, and will, gener[ally] as the representative part of human inner life."[132] The word **spirit** can also refer to evil **spirits** or demons (fallen angels). The question then is whether a particular teaching is sourced in **the Spirit of God** or instead is sourced in the human **spirit** or even demons. The **false prophets** may speak from their own imaginations or **spirits**: "Son of man, prophesy against the prophets of Israel that prophesy, and say thou unto them that prophesy out of their own hearts...the foolish prophets, that follow their own spirit, and have seen nothing!" (Ezekiel 13:2-3) They may also propagate ideas sourced in "seducing spirits, and doctrines of devils." (1 Timothy 4:1)

The litmus for John's readers was, in the first instance, to know the source for truth: **Hereby know ye the Spirit of God: Every spirit that confesseth that Jesus Christ is come in the flesh is of God**. The word **confesseth** is the

---

[132] William Arndt et al., *A Greek-English Lexicon of the New Testament*, 833.

Greek verb ὁμολογέω (homologeō) and in this context means "to concede that something is factual or true, *grant, admit, confess*."[133] To confess **that Jesus Christ is come in the flesh** was to confess both that **Jesus** is in fact the Messiah or **Christ** and that he had **come in the flesh**, i.e., the reality of the incarnation that John addressed in his prologue. We cannot flip this around to conclude that everything a person says is sound doctrine just because he or she says **that Jesus Christ is come in the flesh**. John's point was that this particular confession was sourced in **the Spirit of God**. The person that denied **that Jesus Christ is come in the flesh** denied foundational truths without which there is no Christianity, and such denial marks them as **false prophets** because their denial is not sourced in **the Spirit of God**. In the context of the deceivers John had in mind in his epistle, their rejection of this truth was at the core of their false teaching and would give them away as **false prophets** whose words were not sourced in **the Spirit of God**. At this point some would say we should learn what we can from the **false prophets** by "eating the meat and throwing out the bones," but John flatly rejected that. When the cake is poisoned, it is not possible to eat around the poison. According to John, **every spirit that confesseth not that Jesus Christ is come in the flesh is not of God**. Regardless of whether they might say something that is true, their doctrine and their purpose **is not of God** and must be avoided entirely.

If the rejection **that Jesus Christ is come in the flesh** is not sourced in **God**, then where is it sourced? John explained that this denial of truth **is that spirit of**

---

[133] Ibid., 708.

antichrist, whereof ye have heard that it should come; and even now already is it in the world. John previously told his readers: "Little children, it is the last time: and as ye have heard that antichrist shall come, even now are there many antichrists; whereby we know that it is the last time... Who is a liar but he that denieth that Jesus is the Christ? He is antichrist, that denieth the Father and the Son." (1 John 2:18, 22) As I noted concerning the prior occurrences, the word **antichrist** is the Greek ἀντίχριστος (antikristos) meaning an adversary of the Messiah, and only occurs in First and Second John. These **false prophets** were **antichrists** because they denied and opposed the truth about **Jesus Christ** and the incarnation. We live in the period John called the last time or last hour – the period immediately preceding the return of **Jesus Christ** – and this age will be characterized by many **false prophets** or **antichrists** who deny and oppose the truth about **Jesus Christ**. Their doctrine is sourced in the **spirit of antichrist**, meaning the **spirit** that denies and opposes **Jesus Christ** and quite probably is a reference to Satan.

> **1 John 4:4** Ye are of God, little children, and have overcome them: because greater is he that is in you, than he that is in the world. **5** They are of the world: therefore speak they of the world, and the world heareth them. **6** We are of God: he that knoweth God heareth us; he that is not of God heareth not us. Hereby know we the spirit of truth, and the spirit of error.

In contrast to the antichrists, John assured his **little children** that they **are of God...and have overcome them: because greater is he that is in you, than he that is in the**

world. The Holy **Spirit** was in them, but the "spirit of antichrist" was influencing the deceivers. As a result, John's readers had **overcome** the deceivers. The term **overcome** is the Greek νικάω (nikaō) and means "to win in the face of obstacles, *be victor, conquer, overcome, prevail.*"[134] John's **little children** had in fact conquered or prevailed against the deceivers because of the reality of the indwelling of the Holy **Spirit**. While they were children **of God**, the deceivers were children **of the world** and consequently **speak they of the world, and the world heareth them**. John previously warned his readers about the **world** or world system (2:15-17) that is passing away, that does not know (understand) God or John's readers (3:1), and that may hate his readers (3:13). As previously noted, this **world** system is opposed to God and to His truth-reality, and those **of the world** like the deceivers teach as truth the exact opposite of the truth-reality. They teach non-reality, yet their lies resonate with worldly people, including worldly Christians that don't exercise discernment.

John and the apostles were **of God**, and just as **the world** listens to doctrine sourced in **the world** (**therefore speak they of the world**), so also **he that knoweth God heareth us**, i.e., John and the apostles. Likewise, **he that is not of God heareth not us**. The deceivers rejected John's teaching in preference to the falsities of **the world**, but does this mean all Christians will listen to sound apostolic doctrine? As explained previously (see notes on 2:3), in John's epistle knowing God is not a synonym for being a Christian, but for a deeper level of intimacy and fellowship with **God**. Those in fellowship with God will

---

[134] Ibid., 673.

heareth apostolic doctrine. However, if John believed that Christians only listen to sound doctrine then his warnings about the deceivers were unnecessary. It is precisely because the children of God can be deceived that John exhorted them to test the spirits.

John concluded the subunit (4:1-6) with **hereby know we the spirit of truth, and the spirit of error.** John's word **hereby** means "by this" or "this is how," pointing back to what he just wrote about testing the spirits and listening to apostolic doctrine. The preceding material was critical for his readers to recognize the false prophet by discerning whether a teaching (a spirit) was in fact a **spirit of truth** or **spirit of error.**

Closing

The Bible places a great emphasis on discerning truth from error. In the Old Testament, the people of Israel were instructed to test the prophets and to put them to death if they "turn you away from the Lord your God, which brought you out of the land of Egypt." (Deuteronomy 13:5) In the last days in which we live, discernment will be replaced with apostasy. As Paul wrote: "For the time will come when they will not endure sound doctrine; but after their own lusts shall they heap to themselves teachers, having itching ears; And they shall turn away *their* ears from the truth, and shall be turned unto fables." (2 Timothy 4:3-4) What we are witnessing today is a rapidly changing culture in transition between the post-modern mindset where truth is relative to a post-truth mindset where truth is irrelevant. Facts and reasoned arguments have been replaced with narratives, historical revisionism, and emotionalism. This flawed thinking has made great headway among Christians, validating Paul's words to Timothy. It is therefore all the more incumbent upon us to exercise discernment and test the spirits, whether they speak to us from without the church or within. The spirit of deception abounds, but greater is He who is in us than he who is in the world.

Application Points

MAIN PRINCIPLE: Test what you hear against sound apostolic doctrine, including especially whether the spirit confesses the reality of the incarnation of the Son of God, in order to distinguish truth from lies.

Discussion Questions

1. Why did John say to test the spirits rather than to test what you hear?

2. Why do you think John's litmus for truth and error was whether the person agreed that Jesus Christ had come in the flesh?

3. What are the implications of the spirit of the antichrist already being in the world?

4. John wrote that the antichrists (deceivers) speak of the world, and the world hears them. In practical terms, what determines that a doctrine is from the world?

5. Why could John say that the litmus for the false teachers was whether they listened to John and the apostles or not? Is John's statement arrogant since it makes him the arbiter of truth?

Chapter 11

God Is Love

1 John 4:7-18

The largest unit within First John (2:28-4:18) begins and ends at the bema judgment. This may seem curious at first, but on careful reflection, it could hardly be any other way. The epistle opened with the incarnation and then immediately transitioned to enjoying fellowship with the Father and the Son, which was made possible because of the incarnation. During the incarnation, the Son perfectly declared God, and John confirmed that God is love. That being the case, through the incarnation Jesus put love on display as none had before him, and indeed as none could. His love lesson climaxed at Calvary, and we are expected to have taken good notes. As Jesus' brethren in this world, we are called to put God's love on display, and we can only do that when we walk in fellowship with God and enjoy a mutual sharing with the holy God who is love. When we do this we are lights in the world and our lives of faithfulness please Jesus, resulting in confidence at the bema judgment when we give an account. As we should expect, the marathon run to the bema is love at every step.

Outline

V. THE PRACTICAL OUTWORKING OF LIVING IN FELLOWSHIP WITH GOD (2:28- 4:18)

a. Abiding in God will result in confidence at the bema judgment (2:28)

b. God's children are made visible by their God-righteousness as they abide in God, and the devil's children are made visible by their lack of God-righteousness (2:29-3:10)

c. The world is hostile to righteousness (3:11-18)

d. Those who show God-love for the brethren experience confidence in prayer (3:19- 24)

e. Discern between the Spirit of Truth and Spirit of Error (4:1-6)

f. Love and truth bring fellowship now and confidence at the bema (4:7-18)

   i. Love is sourced in God and failing to love shows we do not know God (4:7-8)

   ii. God's initiating love for us was manifested by sending His Son to be a propitiation for our sins that we might live (4:9-10)

   iii. God's initiating love compels us to love one another and thereby experience God abiding in us and His love completed in us (4:11-12)

   iv. The Spirit of truth assures us of our mutually abiding fellowship with God (4:13)

v.   Those who confess that Jesus is the Son of God experience mutually abiding fellowship with God and know His love (4:14-15)

vi. God is love, and abiding leads to His completed love in us and confidence at the bema (4:16-18)

Scripture and Comments

John revisited the issue of love before closing the inclusio on the bema judgment. To see this as mere repetition misses the point. John wanted his readers to see the connection between love and the bema judgment, but he also wanted to bring his theology of love to its apex with Jesus' love lesson at Calvary.

> **1 John 4:7** Beloved, let us love one another: for love is of God; and every one that loveth is born of God, and knoweth God. **8** He that loveth not knoweth not God; for God is love. **9** In this was manifested the love of God toward us, because that God sent his only begotten Son into the world, that we might live through him. **10** Herein is love, not that we loved God, but that he loved us, and sent his Son *to be* the propitiation for our sins.

John next elaborated (4:7-16) on how Christians recognize that God dwells in them. He earlier stated that his readers may "know that he abideth in us, by the Spirit which he hath given us" (3:24), and at the end of the subunit concluded, "hereby know we that we dwell in him, and he in us, because he hath given us of his Spirit." (1 John 4:13) Between these statements, the emphasis has been love. John exhorted his **beloved** readers, **let us love one**

another. This, of course, "is the message that ye heard from the beginning, that we should love one another." (1 John 3:11) As John earlier stated, "the children of God are manifest" when they do God-righteousness, and this is exemplified in loving others "in deed and in truth." (1 John 3:10-18) Expanding on his earlier statements, John explained that **love is of God, and every one that loveth is born of God, and knoweth God**. True and genuine **love** is sourced in **God**. The world has its counterfeits and so we do well to distinguish the genuine article. As I previously referred to the righteousness of **God** as God-righteousness, I will refer to genuine **love** sourced in **God** as God-love, which is to be distinguished from the distorted secularized concepts of **love**.

With this God-love in mind, it naturally follows that **every one that** exhibits God-love **is born of God, and knoweth God**. To be clear, John did not say that exhibiting God-love is how someone becomes a child **of God**. That is cart before the horse theology. Rather, only those **born of God** are capable of exhibiting God-love, consistent with John's earlier statement that "every one that doeth righteousness is born of him." (1 John 2:29) They are uniquely able to exhibit God-love because God's "seed remaineth in" them. (1 John 3:9) Not only are they **born of God** but they **knoweth God**. As I showed in the notes on First John 2:3, the concept of knowing **God** as John used the term meant an intimate and experiential knowledge of **God**. Accordingly, the person that exhibits God-love is a child of God with a relative level of maturity evidenced by their experiential knowledge and understanding of the character of God.

In contrast to those that exhibit God-love, those that **loveth not knoweth not God**. Christians are as capable as anyone of failing to exhibit God-love, but that failure does not prove that they are fake or spurious Christians. Indeed, if it did, we'd all eventually be found out for what we are not. What it does establish is a lack of experiential knowledge and understanding of the character of **God** because **God is love**. This does not mean that **God is** only **love**. This aspect of the nature and character of **God** is not to the exclusion of His other attributes, such as His justice. It is beyond our purpose here to explore all the attributes or perfections of God, but it is imperative that John's words not be used to distort the character of **God** by arguing that His **love** diminishes or overrides His other attributes. Of human beings, we might say that they are loving because they do deeds of **love**, but with **God**, He does deeds of **love** because He **is love**. This is a part of the essential nature of His being, and to know God intimately necessarily means we have an experiential knowledge and understanding of His character, including God-love.

The way in which the **love of God toward us** was revealed or **manifested** was that **God sent his only begotten Son into the world, that we might live through him**. When John wrote **herein is love** he sought to explain that God is the source and initiator of God-love. It is **not that we loved God**. Indeed, we could never do so on our own. Rather, it is **that God loved us, and sent his Son to be the propitiation for our sins**. Apart from the life-giving work of Jesus Christ at Calvary to address our sin problem, we would not be children of God with His seed in us enabling God-love. **God** showed His **love** first and in the ultimate way by sending **his Son** Jesus Christ. John previously wrote that Jesus "is the propitiation for our sins, and not for ours only, but also for the sins of the whole world." (1 John 2:2) The word **propitiation** in 2:2 and here is the

Greek ἱλασμός (hilasmos) and means an "appeasement necessitated by sin."[135] Jesus' sacrifice on a Roman cross provided the satisfaction of God's holy requirements as to our sin, and no greater demonstration of **love**, and no greater proof that **God is love**, was possible.

> **I John 4:11** Beloved, if God so loved us, we ought also to love one another. **12** No man hath seen God at any time. If we love one another, God dwelleth in us, and his love is perfected in us. **13** Hereby know we that we dwell in him, and he in us, because he hath given us of his Spirit.

That **God so loved us** by sending His Son to be a propitiation for our sins should motivate our love toward our brethren – **we ought also to love one another**. This matter of showing God-love toward others is how we **know** we are experiencing a mutual abiding between **God** and **us**. As John explained, **no man hath seen God at any time**. Recall that John wrote elsewhere in reference to the incarnation: "No man hath seen God at any time; the only begotten Son, which is in the bosom of the Father, he hath declared him." (John 1:18) Before Jesus completed his earthly ministry and ascended to the Father, he promised to send the Holy Spirit. (John 16:7) John's readers and Christians today need to understand that **if we love one another** – again, with God-love and not any worldly counterfeits – we experience **God** dwelling or abiding **in us, and his love is perfected** or made complete **in us**. His **perfected love in us** confirms the mutually abiding relationship, so that we **know that we dwell** or abide / remain **in God, and he in us**. And this **perfected love** can be experientially realized and

---

[135] William Arndt et al., *A Greek-English Lexicon of the New Testament*, 474.

expressed **because he hath given us of his Spirit**. When we experience this **perfected love** we know **his Spirit** is working in us and that we are enjoying mutual abiding fellowship with the Holy God who is light and in whom is no darkness. (1 John 1:5) This **perfected love** is no secret or hidden **love** but is practical and visible to those around us.

> **1 John 4:14** And we have seen and do testify that the Father sent the Son *to be* the Saviour of the world. **15** Whosoever shall confess that Jesus is the Son of God, God dwelleth in him, and he in God. **16** And we have known and believed the love that God hath to us. God is love; and he that dwelleth in love dwelleth in God, and God in him.

Continuing from the prior verses about **we**, i.e., John and his readers, not seeing God but nevertheless experiencing mutual abiding fellowship with God when they exhibit God-love for one another, John concluded that **we have seen and do testify that the Father sent the Son to be the Saviour of the world**. As John already stated, God was the initiator of love by sending His Son to be a propitiation for our sin (4:10), and thus **the Saviour of the world**. That love is now perfected in believers by the Holy Spirit as they experience the abiding relationship with God. John opened his epistle with his recollection of the incarnation of the Son, whom he saw and later testified about. Now John and his readers who were abiding in fellowship with God were also in fellowship with one another (1:3) and testified together about **the Father** sending **the Son to be the Saviour of the world**. With the deceivers in view, John added that **whosoever shall confess** or agree **that Jesus is the Son of God, God dwelleth in him, and he in God.**

Notably, John wrote **Jesus is** and not **Jesus** was, because the **Saviour of the world** died on a cross but didn't stay dead. This confession was the essential litmus for fellowship with John and the other apostles and with **God**. No doubt the deceivers denied **that Jesus is the Son of God.** Whatever they made **Jesus** out to be, the deceivers would not permit that he **is the Son of God**, fully human and fully deity.

In contrast to the deceivers, John and his readers **have known and believed the love that God hath to us** by sending **the Son to be the Saviour of the world**. Repeating his words from 4:8, **God is love.** One cannot have fellowship or abide in a holy **God** with sin. One cannot have fellowship or abide in a **God** who **is love** without mutually sharing in perfected love. Nor can someone out of fellowship show perfected God-love to others. Accordingly, John concluded that **he that dwelleth** or abides **in love dwelleth** or abides **in God, and God in him**. This is fellowship, a primary focus of the entire epistle – not tests for life. **Love** is the critical key, empowered by the Spirit, made possible by **Jesus** providing the propitiation so that we could be God's children with His seed remaining in us. Without **love**, there is neither fellowship nor maturity nor an empowerment of the Spirit. As the apostle Paul concluded: "And now abideth faith, hope, charity [love], these three; but the greatest of these is charity [love]." (1 Corinthians 13:3)

> **1 John 4:17** Herein is our love made perfect, that we may have boldness in the day of judgment: because as he is, so are we in this world.

John previously wrote that those who keep God's Word have the **love** of God perfected in them (2:5) and that when we **love** one another God abides in us and His **love** is perfected in us (4:12). When John wrote **herein is our love made perfect** or complete, it was the corporate experience (hence **our**) of perfected **love** that results from mutually abiding with God, or fellowship with God in the prior verse (4:16) that was in view. John started this unit in 2:28 with the exhortation to "abide in him" or live in fellowship with God so "that when he shall appear, we may have confidence, and not be ashamed before him at his coming." As I suggested in the notes there, John had the bema judgment in mind when Christians give an account before Jesus in relation to rewards and inheritance, not eternal destiny.

As John neared the end of the central theological unit of his epistle (2:28-4:19), he came full circle. Those who abide in fellowship with God experience perfected **love** toward one another, and this provides confidence or **boldness in the day of judgment**. Note that the KJV used "confidence" in 2:28 and **boldness** in 4:17, but they are the same Greek noun παρρησία (parrēsia) which means "a state of boldness and confidence, *courage, confidence, boldness, fearlessness,* esp[ecially] in the presence of persons of high rank."[136] The opposite would be to experience shame (2:28) when we stand before Jesus and give an account. A life in the light of fellowship and perfected love leads to **boldness** at the bema judgment **because as he is, so are we in this world**. God is love, and we are to be like Him **in this world** with our testimony about the Son and demonstration of God-love to others

---

[136] Ibid., 781.

"in deed and in truth" (3:18). That is the life of true success that ushers us into the presence of Jesus Christ at the bema with **boldness** and not shame.

> **1 John 4:18** There is no fear in love; but perfect love casteth out fear: because fear hath torment. He that feareth is not made perfect in love.

The context of these verses is still the bema judgment referenced in 4:17. Here, John added to his prior statement that perfected **love** produces confidence or boldness at the bema. This begs the question of what might preclude or diminish that confidence. We need to bear in mind that the bema judgment assesses our faithfulness with a view to rewards, not whether we are children of God. The latter was settled at the moment of faith, and on that point, John repeatedly affirmed his belief that his dear friends and little children were children of God. John explained that **fear** is inconsistent with **love**, that is, the **love** sourced in the character of God that I have referred to as God-love in the earlier notes. Just as God is light and in Him is no darkness at all, we are to understand that God is love (4:16), and consequently, in Him **is no fear** at all. When we abide in God or walk in fellowship with God we experience a mutual sharing with His character, and especially His complete and fearless **love**. When that happens, our own **fear** falls away, because **perfect love casteth out fear**. The **fear** in view is rooted in doubts and uncertainties we may have about the bema based on how we have lived.

John continued by observing that **fear hath torment**. His point was not that Christians would experience **torment** or punishment at the bema. Rather, without the perfected

love that accompanies mutually abiding with God and removes **fear**, we will experience **fear** as a part of our daily walk. John could not have been more explicit: **He that feareth is not made perfect in love**. The Christian with fear is **not made perfect in love** and thus not experiencing fellowship with the **God** who is **love** and has no **fear**. He or she lives with **fear** and is in danger of not having boldness at the bema. But what is it that we are afraid of? The confidence or boldness we can experience at the bema is an outgrowth of the confidence we can experience daily as we walk in fellowship and express perfected **love** with our lives. This intimacy and mutual sharing with **God** is what we were made for. This is God's will for us, and anything less is to be out of His will for us at the moment. When we are in fellowship we enjoy an experiential knowledge of **God**, His **perfect love** which we then channel to others, and the experienced righteousness that visibly manifests us as His children. This is the kind of knowledge that removes all the doubts and fears that our minds, the world, and the devil throw at us. When we are not in fellowship, we are still the children of **God** and should know that based on God's Word (e.g., John 3:16), but we are susceptible to doubts and fears about standing before Jesus at the bema judgment. At the same time, while we are out of fellowship, we are far more susceptible to confusion and deceptions and may not comprehend why we are experiencing fear. That's why John earlier called this experience death, and here in this passage it is called **torment**.

Closing

The bema judgment should be taken seriously. If we believe we will stand before Jesus and give an account of our lives – and the Bible unequivocally affirms we will – that is a sobering reality that may produce fear, especially if we know that we've squandered our time on worldly pursuits. God doesn't want us to live in fear. We cannot live life in reverse, but we can resolve to abide in God going forward. When we do that, we can count on God's promise that His love will be perfected in us. This will transform us from the inside out and will be manifested in how we relate to other people. In the process, the mature love we experience will replace our doubts and fears with confidence.

Application Points

- MAIN PRINCIPLE: God showed us what love is by sending His Son to be a propitiation for our sins so that we might live through him, and this display of love should motivate our love for one another, which will result in His perfected love in us, the casting out of our fears and doubts, and confidence at the bema judgment.

- We know that we are experiencing mutually abiding fellowship with God by the Holy Spirit given to us.

Discussion Questions

1. What does it mean that Jesus is the propitiation for our sins?

2. What is the connection between God's display of love for us through the Son and how we should relate to others?

3. How can Jesus be the "savior of the world" (4:14) if it turns out that not everyone gets saved?

4. What is the difference between saying God is love and saying God does loving things?

5. What is the relationship between John's statements that God is light and God is love?

6. How are we like Jesus in the world?

Chapter 12

Conquering the World
1 John 4:19-5:21

John's epistle was occasioned by the dangers of false teachers he labeled as antichrists because they denied the incarnation of the Son of God. Before John explicitly addressed the antichrists for the first time, he grounded the epistle on the incarnation, set out principles of fellowship, and provided assurance to his readers that their sins were forgiven, they know the Father and the Son, and they have overcome the devil. Only after all of that did John expressly warn his readers about the allures of the world system and the deceptions of the world's apostles who denied the truth. That was followed by the central exhortation of First John – that his readers would abide in fellowship with God. In one way or another, this was the key to everything, including withstanding the antichrists. John's final major unit closed by retracing his steps in a way that would further encourage and fortify his readers as overcomers who could enjoy fellowship with God, and bring his epistle full circle. He grounded his final unit on the reality of the incarnation just as he had opened his epistle with the incarnation. The closing verses re-affirmed the centrals truths his readers could know and a timely warning about idols.

Outline

VI. EXPERIENTIAL ASSURANCE AS OVERCOMERS (4:19-5:20)

    a. Our faith is the victory (4:19-5:4)

        i. The truth-reality is that one cannot simultaneously love God and not love the brethren (4:19-21)

        ii. Those who believe Jesus is the Christ are God's children and love the Father and the Son (5:1)

        iii. We know we love God's children when we love God and obey His commands (5:2)

        iv. We love God by obeying, but obedience is not burdensome because those born of God conquer the world through faith (5:3-4)

        v. The overcomers are those that believe Jesus is the Son of God (5:5)

    b. Our victory is grounded in the incarnation (5:6-13)

        i. Jesus Christ came by the water and the blood and that reality is confirmed by the Spirit, the water and the blood (5:6-8)

        ii. God testifies to the truth-reality about His Son, and those that reject that truth make God a liar (5:9-10)

    iii. God testifies that we have eternal life in His Son, and the one without the Son does not have life (5:11-12)

    iv. If we believe in the name of the Son of God, we know that we have eternal life (5:13)

  c. Overcomers have confidence in prayer (5:14-17)

    i. Overcomers are confident about receiving what is requested in prayer according to God's will (5:14-15)

    ii. Overcomers pray for a brother in a sin not unto death, but understand that prayer for a brother in a sin unto death will not be granted (5:16-17)

  d. Overcomers know the truth-reality (5:18-20)

    i. God's children don't sin and are impervious to the devil (5:18)

    ii. The world is under the influence and control of the devil (5:19)

    iii. God's Son has given us understanding of the truth so that we can know and abide in the Son, who is the true God and eternal life (5:20)

  e. Stay away from idols (5:21)

Scripture and Comments

The previous major unit was the large inclusio (2:28-4:18) that started and ended on the issue of confidence at the bema. The final unit brought his readers (and us) back to the reality of the incarnation the antichrists denied.

1 John 4:19 We love him, because he first loved us. 20 If a man say, I love God, and hateth his brother, he is a liar: for he that loveth not his brother whom he hath seen, how can he love God whom he hath not seen? 21 And this commandment have we from him, That he who loveth God love his brother also.

Up to this point, John focused on his readers loving one another. Next, the focus was moved from loving others to loving God. John wrote that **we love** God **because he first loved us.** In view of the fact that God is **love**, and we can only experience perfected **love** through fellowship with the **God** who is **love**, it is unsurprising that our **love** for God is sourced in and made possible by His **love** for us. Also, His **love** is the model for what **love** is and what it is not. It is pure and unadulterated with any speck of hate for His children. That God **first loved us** has implications. If a person claims to **love God** in the true sense of the God-love that is maximal in His character, but **hateth his brother, he is a liar.** John used the term **liar** previously (1:10, 2:4, 2:22) for those whose claims were inconsistent with reality as understood by God's character and Word. **Love** with some hate mixed in is not **love** at all no matter the label attached to it, and certainly not God-love. For one child of God to **hateth** another child of God establishes that at that moment there is an absence of **love** for God, despite all claims to the contrary. When we grasp the concept of God-love, John's point is logically compelling. **For he that loveth not his brother whom he hath seen, how can he love God whom he hath not seen?** The answer demanded by John's question is that he cannot. It is an impossibility, but the **commandment we** have from him is that he who loveth God loveth his brother also. If we are doing the former, we will necessarily do the latter. If we don't do the latter, we are not doing the former in that moment. This is the danger of falling out of fellowship.

> 1 John 5:1 Whosoever believeth that Jesus is the Christ is born of God: and every one that loveth him that begat loveth him also that is begotten of him.

Despite the chapter break, it is apparent that John continued building on the immediately preceding verses (4:19-21) concerning love. As usual, his logic was simple and compelling. First, anyone that **believeth that Jesus is the Christ** or Messiah **is born of God**. John could not be any more emphatic about what is required to be a Christian: (1) faith or belief (2) that Jesus (3) is **the Christ**. It is the greatest irony that so many attempt a theological hijacking of this epistle and insist that John provided as his litmus for true or genuine Christians various performance metrics. Indeed, John insisted, as the apostle Paul did (see Romans 3-4), in faith alone without works, commitments, promises, down payments or balloon payments.

While John insisted on faith without fine print, many would alter the definitions of words to avoid the consistent "faith alone" witness of the entire New Testament. They argue faith means believing plus commitments and balloon payments and repentance of sins and the like. We are entitled to our private opinions but not our private definitions. No Greek lexicon supports this pre-loading of the word "faith" so that its true meaning is "not faith." It is disingenuous to say "faith alone" while saying faith includes works. Moreover, if John (and Jesus and Paul) had wanted to teach that one need only believe, and not "believe plus," they would have used exactly the words we see repeatedly throughout the New Testament.

As John had much to say about loving our fellow Christians, it was critical that he identify who those people are in as simple a way as possible. No doubt John had the deceivers in mind whose twisted doctrines called into question who the true or genuine Christians are. Those antichrists might even argue that if someone who professes to be a Christian doesn't fit their artificially imposed additional criteria, then that person need not be loved. John made it easy – those who have placed faith in **Jesus** as **the Christ** are children **of God**. With that foundation established, John added that **every one that loveth him that begat loveth him also that is begotten of him**. In other words, everyone that loves God loves His children. Those who love God will keep the command of 4:21, "That he who loveth God love his brother also." As explored with regard to 4:20, we cannot love God and not love His children because of the very source and nature of God-love. At the risk of being repetitive, John did not say that we must love God's children to become a Christian or prove we are one. Only Christians in fellowship with God are capable of God-love, and so love's absence reflects an absence of fellowship at that moment and not that one is lost.

Before leaving this verse, I point out that there is controversy about this verse because some interpret it to mean that regeneration precedes faith. The controversy centers on the verb **is born**. The word **born** is the Greek γεννάω (gennaō) and means "become the parent of, *beget*."[137] Here, John used the perfect tense, indicating a

---

[137] William Arndt et al., *A Greek-English Lexicon of the New Testament*, 193.

past completed action with continuing consequences. His point was simply that whoever presently believes **that Jesus is the Christ** was **born of God** from the first moment of that faith and their status as a child of God continues to the present. Thus, it is faith that results in being born again, not the other way around. This is consistent with the overwhelming witness of the New Testament that makes salvation depend on faith alone.

Some Reform theologians argue that a person is born again or regenerated then later exercises faith. This position is based on a theological commitment, sometimes called Calvinism after the Reformer John Calvin, that people have zero role in salvation. According to Calvinism, (1) humanity in its lostness or depravity cannot believe the gospel or even understand it, (2) before God created the universe He selected a small subset of humanity to save called the elect and did not select the others, (3) at Calvary Jesus died solely for the elect and completely secured their salvation at that time, (4) at a moment of God's choosing He irresistibly draws or efficaciously calls (i.e., regenerates) the elect person making them born again and then gives them faith, and (5) the elect necessarily persevere in faith and good works until they die. I have presented here in summary form traditional Calvinism, but not all modern Calvinists hold to all of these points. If you want to dig further on this issue, I refer you to my book *Deconstructing Calvinism.* I would add that these five points did not originate with John Calvin. For further information on the origins of Calvinism, I recommend church historian Ken Wilson's book *Foundations of Augustinian Calvinism.* The main point of briefly chasing this rabbit is that traditional Calvinists insist on regeneration before faith, and must do so for logical consistency because of their view of depravity – that lost people cannot believe the gospel without God first regenerating them and giving them faith. Neither John nor any other New Testament writer taught this doctrine.

> **1 John 5:2** By this we know that we love the children of God, when we love God, and keep his commandments. **3** For this is the love of God, that we keep his commandments: and his commandments are not grievous.

When Jesus was asked what the greatest commandment was, he responded: "The first of all the commandments *is*, Hear, O Israel; The Lord our God is one Lord: And thou shalt love the Lord thy God with all thy heart, and with all thy soul, and with all thy mind, and with all thy strength: this *is* the first commandment. And the second *is* like, *namely* this, Thou shalt love thy neighbour as thyself. There is none other commandment greater than these." (Mark 12:29-31) If the greatest commandments are grounded in love for God and others, it stands to reason that love cannot be separated from obedience in general. John connected the two in order to provide assurance to his readers that they were in fact carrying out the great commandment to love one another. He wrote, **by this we know that we love the children of God, when we love God, and keep his commandments**. John already told his readers that they cannot **love God** without loving His children also, but what exactly does it mean to **love God**? What is God's **love** language? Simply put, it is obedience.

John explained, **this is the love of God, that we keep his commandments**. Some have assumed that this means the Old Testament commands under the Law of Moses, including the Ten Commandments. The problem with this thinking is that Jesus inaugurated the New Covenant at the cross, and so the commands in view are those under the New Covenant. It is true that some Mosaic Covenant commands are also part of the New Covenant, but those commands are narrowed applications of the command to love. For example, if we love another person, we won't steal from them, bear false witness about them, or covet their stuff or their spouse. Many of the Mosaic Covenant commands are not part of the New Covenant, including for example the dietary restrictions, various feasts, and animal sacrifices. Some will point out that the Mosaic Covenant included loving our neighbor (Leviticus 19:18), but the day before his crucifixion Jesus provided an updated love command that he specifically referred to as his command: "This is my commandment, That ye love one another, as I have loved you." (John 15:12) This new command of loving others *in the manner with which Jesus loved his disciples* is part of the New Covenant. It was during this same conversation that Jesus told the eleven, "If ye love me, keep my commandments." (John 14:15) Thus, love and obedience are inseparable. Jesus then related obedience to abiding in love: "If ye keep my commandments, ye shall abide in my love; even as I have kept my Father's commandments, and abide in his love." (John 15:10) John relied on Jesus' words when he also equated loving God with obedience.

John's final comment is that God's **commandments are not grievous** or burdensome. Jesus criticized the Pharisees for placing "heavy burdens" (Matthew 23:4) on the people's shoulders while they ignored the "weightier matters of the law, judgment, mercy, and faith" (Matthew 23:23). In contrast, Jesus explained that his "yoke is easy" and his "burden is light." (Matthew 11:30) John's word

grievous is the term Jesus used that is translated "heavy" and "weightier." John assured his readers that God's **commandments are not** a heavy weight on their shoulders. The reason is that the **commandments** center on various applications of **love**, and that should not be burdensome for a person "born of God." John's comment provided a fitting transition between the current subunit (4:20-5:3) and the next (5:4-17), which focused on what empowers Christian living.

> 1 John 5:4 For whatsoever is born of God overcometh the world: and this is the victory that overcometh the world, *even* our faith.
> 5 Who is he that overcometh the world, but he that believeth that Jesus is the Son of God?

Building on why the commandments are not burdensome (the **for** has the sense of "because"), John stated that **whatsoever is born of God overcometh the world**. The word **overcometh** translates the Greek verb νικάω (nikaō), which means "to win in the face of obstacles, *be victor, conquer, overcome, prevail.*"[138] Obviously, if Christians have overcome or conquered **the world**, keeping God's commands should not be burdensome. But we should note that John used the word **whatsoever** not "whosoever." The word "whosoever" (see 5:1) is a masculine adjective, but **whatsoever** is a neuter adjective, suggesting John had something and not someone in mind. While I would not be dogmatic about why John departed from his typical "whosoever" in favor of **whatsoever**, I believe the key is in 3:9: "Whosoever is born of god doth not commit sin; for his seed remaineth in him: and he cannot sin, because he is born of God." I argued in the

---

[138] Ibid., 673.

notes for 3:9 that the seed gives us a new nature, and while we still retain the old nature as well, we are capable of living out the new nature and when we do, we do not sin. The word "seed" (Greek sperma) is a neuter noun, and here John emphasized that the "seed" that makes it possible for Christians to live righteously (3:9-10) is that part of us that **overcometh the world.**

John added, **this is the victory that overcometh the world, even our faith.** When we come to the word **faith** in the Scriptures, we must remember that **faith** always has content. The Bible does not call upon us to have **faith** in some ambiguous or abstract sense. Many non-Christians with all kinds of beliefs may employ the word **faith** as if this is a power source or guiding light in itself without any specific content. For the Christian, **faith** must be in someone or something, and the interpreter cannot blindly assume what that content is in a given passage. Remember, **faith** is the noun form for the verb "believe" and its use always demands that we determine from context, not presumption or guessing, what the content of the **faith** is. Here, John was explicit when he asked rhetorically, **Who is he that overcometh the world, but he that believeth that Jesus is the Son of God?** The content of the **faith** that **overcometh the world** is that **Jesus is the Son of God.**

The deceivers / antichrists denied the Father and the Son (2:22) and we know that the one that denies the Son does not have the Father (2:23). John previously stated that "whosoever shall confess that Jesus is the Son of God, God dwelleth in him, and he in God." (1 John 4:15) As I noted regarding 4:15, the confession of truth that **Jesus is the Son of God** was the essential litmus for fellowship with John and the other apostles and with **God.** The deceivers denied **that Jesus is the Son of God** because they rejected the incarnation. Whatever they made **Jesus** out to be, the deceivers would not confess that he **is the Son of God**, fully human and fully deity. John's readers had **faith that Jesus is the Son of God** and so had the victory over **the world** system and its elitist antichrists who touted superior knowledge but were ultimately the voice of **the world** system and not overcomers.

> **1 John 5:6** This is he that came by water and blood, *even* Jesus Christ; not by water only, but by water and blood. And it is the Spirit that beareth witness, because the Spirit is truth.

Having reaffirmed the confession that "Jesus is the Son of God," John elaborated of Jesus that **this is he that came by water and blood, even Jesus Christ; not by water only, but by water and blood.** While John never attempted to itemize all that the deceivers taught, we know they denied that "Jesus is the Son of God." They did not deny **Jesus** existed, but denied that he was God in the flesh, likely indicative of a Gnostic or pre-gnostic notion that all flesh is evil and so the Son of God could never be corporeal. The Gnostics and others, including a man named Cerinthus who is believed to have opposed John, believed a divine being entered the human **Jesus** at his baptism but abandoned him before he died on the cross. With this context, we can understand John's insistence that **Jesus** is the **Christ** or Messiah and that he **came by water and blood**. These, of course, were the bookends of Jesus' earthly ministry, his baptism and crucifixion, and by implication everything in between was included. That John likely had in mind deceivers who accepted the **water** but denied the **blood** is shown by John's insistence that **Jesus** did not come **by water only, but by water and blood.** The Son of God's ministry included the cross.

Zane Hodges astutely observes of this passage: "The baptism of Jesus should be given its full significance here. In the New Testament it is evidently the formal inauguration of Jesus as the messianic Savior, i.e., as the Christ."[139] John's Gospel explained the ministry of John the Baptizer who "bear witness of that light, that all men through him might believe." (John 1:7) John was emphatic that "the word was made flesh, and dwelt among us, (and we beheld his glory, the glory as the only begotten of the Father,) full of grace and truth." (John 1:14) John the Baptizer identified Jesus (John 1:15) and while baptizing in the Jordan River (John 1:28) saw Jesus and exclaimed: "Behold the Lamb of God, which taketh away the sin of the world." (John 1:29) Critically for the current passage in First John, the Baptizer testified that he "saw the Spirit descending from heaven like a dove, and it abode on" Jesus. (John 1:32) He further explained: "I knew him not: but he that sent me to baptize with water, the same said unto me, Upon whom thou shalt see the Spirit descending, and remaining on him, the same is he which baptizeth with the Holy Ghost. And I saw, and bare record that this is the Son of God." (John 1:33-34) At Jesus' baptism, the Holy **Spirit** confirmed to John the Baptizer that Jesus is none other than the Son of God and the saviour that would "taketh away the sin of the world." Back in First John, we read that **it is the Spirit that beareth witness, because the Spirit is truth.** When Jesus **came by water** the **Spirit** confirmed the reality of who Jesus is, the very reality the deceivers denied.

---

[139] Zane Clark Hodges, *The Epistle of John*, 219.

At this point, we must ask, who is to be believed? The voice of the world or **the Spirit**? John stated that **the Spirit is truth**, a phrasing similar to his earlier statement that "God is love" (4:8, 16). It is not that **the Spirit** merely says true things, but that **the Spirit is truth** by absolute and maximal character and nature. Jesus referred to the Holy **Spirit** as "the Spirit of truth" (John 14:17, 15:26, 16:13) "which proceedeth from the Father, he shall testify of me" and "he will guide you into all truth: for he shall not speak of himself; but whatsoever he shall hear, that shall he speak." The Holy **Spirit** is the third member of the triune God, proceeds from the Father, and is of the same nature as the Father and the Son. Throughout the Bible, God is associated with truth, and the Son of God claimed to be "the truth" (John 14:6) as he anticipated his crucifixion and the close of his earthly ministry and promised to send the Holy **Spirit** of truth. In short, there could be no more reliable witness to the reality of Jesus Christ than the Holy **Spirit**. The deceivers disputed the crucifixion of the Son of God and by inference the sufficiency of the cross. The Holy Spirit affirmed who Jesus was, and John rebutted the deceivers with the affirmation that "he is the propitiation for our sins" and that God "sent his Son to be the propitiation for our sins." (1 John 2:2, 4:10)

> **1 John 5:7** For there are three that bear record in heaven, the Father, the Word, and the Holy Ghost: and these three are one. **8** And there are three that bear witness in earth, the Spirit, and the water, and the blood: and these three agree in one.

These verses have been at the center of controversy because in nearly all Greek manuscripts verse 7 only says "for there are three that bear record" and verse 8 only says "the Spirit, and the water, and the blood: and these three agree in one." It is beyond the scope of this book to deep dive how the words "in heaven, the Father, the Word, and the Holy Ghost: and these three are one. And there are three that bear witness in earth" (sometimes called the Johannine Comma) appear in KJV. For a more fulsome discussion I refer the reader to F.F. Bruce's comments in his commentary on First John, which I only summarize here.[140] The first known manuscript with some of these words was a Fifth Century Latin manuscript. The words were later included in the Latin Vulgate (c. AD 800). When Erasmus (a Catholic) published his Greek New Testament in 1516, he was criticized by some for excluding the Johannine Comma, but defended his position because of their absence from any Greek manuscripts. Shortly after, a new Greek manuscript created around 1520 was provided to Erasmus to persuade him to add the words to his Greek New Testament. Although he knew the added words had simply been translated from the Vulgate, and not a Greek manuscript, he reluctantly included them in a later edition of his Greek New Testament and alluded to the issue in a footnote. From his influential Greek New Testament, the words were included in Tyndale's translation and other print editions of the Greek New Testament relied upon by the KJV translators. The interested reader should do their own study and come to their own conviction based on the empirical evidence and not a theological commitment one way or the other.

With this brief excursus in mind, John's words as presented in the KJV are unquestionably true. In Jewish thinking, two witnesses were required to establish a

---

[140] F. F. Bruce, *The Epistles of John*, 129–130.

matter in court. (Deuteronomy 17:6, 19:15; John 8:17-18) But here we have **three that bear record in heaven, the Father, the Word, and the Holy Ghost: and these three are one**. The reference to **the Word** reflects how John presented Jesus in the opening of the Fourth Gospel as **the Word** or the logos: "In the beginning was the Word, and the Word was with God, and the Word was God. The same was in the beginning with God. All things were made by him; and without him was not any thing made that was made." (John 1:1-3) In John's Gospel, Jesus cited three witnesses of who he is, namely John the Baptizer, his own works, and the Father's testimony in the scriptures. (John 5:31-40) Here in First John, the Holy Spirit's witness that Jesus came by the water and the blood is affirmed by the triune God **in heaven** as well as **three...in earth**.

It may strike us as odd that the three witnesses **in earth** are **the Spirit, and the water, and the blood: and these three agree in one**. It is apparent from John's Gospel that **the Spirit** testified to the truth of **the water and the blood**, but how can **the water and the blood** be witnesses of themselves? Many modern apologists (e.g., William Lane Craig, *On Guard: Defending Your Faith with Reason and Precision*; Michael Licona and Gary Habermas, *The Case for the Resurrection of Jesus*) ably demonstrate that the resurrection is thoroughly attested from the historic record. Indeed, it may be shown that the resurrection is, among key events in ancient history, far better attested than many of the facts skeptics readily accept about other ancient figures such as the Roman emperors. In John's day, there were still living witnesses of the events of Jesus' life, and many others who heard from those witnesses. At that time, those events were more or less beyond any reasonable doubt, and in that sense **the water and the blood** had their own historical legs to stand on. The deceivers, like many today, had little interest in historical facts and records.

> **1 John 5:9** If we receive the witness of men, the witness of God is greater: for this is the witness of God which he hath testified of his Son.

John called upon his readers to carefully consider whose witness carries more weight. In modern day jury trials, the jurors are entrusted with the task of not blindly believing testimony, but assessing credibility. John's readers were entrusted with this same task: **If we receive the witness of men, the witness of God is greater**. As Paul wrote, "let God be true, but every man a liar." (Romans 3:4) **God is the greater** or more credible witness than the human deceivers and so His testimony should be received and the deceivers' witness rejected. **God** provided the heavenly witness, and the deceivers provided a voice for the corrupt world system. And the **witness of God which he hath testified of his Son** affirmed that he came by the water and the blood. At the baptism, God testified: "This is my beloved Son, in whom I am well pleased." (Matthew 3:17) At the transfiguration, He again testified: "This is my beloved Son, in whom I am well pleased; hear ye him." (Matthew 17:5; see also 2 Peter 1:16-18) After the cross: "But God raised him from the dead: And he was seen many days of them which came up with him from Galilee to Jerusalem, who are his witnesses unto the people. And we declare unto you glad tidings, how that the promise which was made unto the fathers, God hath fulfilled the same unto us their children, in that he hath raised up

Jesus again; as it is also written in the second psalm, Thou art my Son, this day have I begotten thee." (Acts 13:30-33)

> **1 John 5:10** He that believeth on the Son of God hath the witness in himself: he that believeth not God hath made him a liar; because he believeth not the record that God gave of his Son. **11** And this is the record, that God hath given to us eternal life, and this life is in his Son. **12** He that hath the Son hath life; *and* he that hath not the Son of God hath not life.

John did not state God's testimony or **record** until 5:11, but first set forth the litmus in 5:10. **He that believeth on** or in **the Son of God hath the witness** of God **in himself.** That testimony or **record** is **that God hath given to us eternal life, and this life is in his Son.** Within the Fourth Gospel, the phrase "believed on him" (John 2:11, 8:31), "believe in him" (John 7:5), and similar variants (e.g., "believed in his name" (John 2:23)) indicate saving faith, or when used negatively, the failure to come to saving faith in Jesus (e.g., John 8:24). As I noted previously, faith must have content. To believe in / on him or in his name points to the person and works of Christ. We read in John 20:31: "But these are written that ye might believe that Jesus is the Christ, the Son of God; and that believing ye might have life through his name." To believe that Jesus is the Christ or Messiah points to his work on the cross. To believe that Jesus is the Son of God points to his divine nature and the incarnation. The present tense "is" (not was) implies the resurrection. Some have argued that the content of faith in John, and here in First John 5:10-11, is **eternal life.** That is, they argue that saving faith is believing the promise of eternal life. That proposition is never stated in John or First John. Rather, it is faith **on** or in **the Son of God** that is saving, and by such faith we freely receive **eternal life**. This **eternal life** is the same **life in his Son**. It is the same **life** Jesus talked about when he said, "I am come that they might have life, and that they might have it more abundantly." (John 10:10) Recall John's earlier words that "God sent his only begotten Son into the world, that we might live through him." (1 John 4:9) Because **eternal life** is in the **Son**, John logically added, **he that hath the Son hath life**. There is no plan B.

John also stated the negative: **he that believeth not God hath made him a liar; because he believeth not the record that God gave his Son.** No doubt John had the deceivers in mind, who likely rejected that John and his readers had eternal life as a result of their faith **on** or in **the Son of God**. Such rejection is not surprising given that the deceivers "confess not that Jesus Christ is come in the flesh." (2 John 7) They "denieth that Jesus is the Christ" (2:22) and "denieth the Son" (2:23). By so denying Jesus, they deny the testimony of **God**, appraising **God** Himself to lack credibility as a witness, and therefore **hath made** God **a liar** because they **believeth not the record that God gave** about **his Son**. Moreover, John confirmed that **he that hath not the Son of God hath not life**. While John stopped short of expressly stating that the deceivers don't have **eternal life**, he could not have been more emphatic that a person must have both the **Son** and **life**, or have neither, without any gray area.

> **1 John 5:13** These things have I written unto you that believe on the name of the Son of God; that ye may know that ye have eternal

life, and that ye may believe on the name of
the Son of God.

John concluded the subunit (5:6-12) with another purpose
statement. As we have already seen, John frequently used
what we should consider as interim purpose statements
intended to characterize a portion of the epistle and not
the entire epistle. Such is the case here: **These things have
I written unto you that believe on the name of the Son of
God; that ye may know that ye have eternal life, and that
ye may believe on the name of the Son of God.** John
previously made clear his understanding that his readers
were Christians and, indeed, overcomers. (1 John 2:12-14)
He repeatedly referred to them as his "beloved" and "little
children," but having said all those things and well aware
of the twisted beliefs of the deceivers that might sow
doubt even among his "little children," John wanted to
give them further affirmation. His reference to **these
things** was not to the entire epistle, but only the
immediately preceding verses 6-12 concerning the
testimony that Jesus came by the water and the blood. To
provide further affirmation to his readers, he addressed
them as **you that believe on the name of the Son of God**.
According to John, those that believed **may know** or be
assured **that ye have eternal life**.

There was also a second reason John wrote **these things**.
In addition to providing further assurance, he wanted to
exhort his readers to continue to **believe on the name of
the Son of God**. This exhortation makes little sense if
John was talking about eternal life since he already
confirmed that promise. This continuing belief or trust
ties to John's next point concerning confidence in prayer.

1 John 5:14 And this is the confidence that we have in him, that, if we ask any thing according to his will, he heareth us: **15** And if we know that he hear us, whatsoever we ask, we know that we have the petitions that we desired of him.

Building on the foundation that his readers believed in "the name of the Son of God," John turned to the issue of **confidence** in prayer. This was not a new topic as John touched on prayer in 3:20-22 where he linked **confidence** in prayer to "keep[ing] his commandments, and do[ing] those things that are pleasing in his sight." Here, John stated that **this is the confidence that we have in him, that, if we ask any thing according to his will, he heareth us.** Jesus told his disciples in John 16:23-24: "Verily, verily, I say unto you, Whatsoever ye shall ask the Father in my name, he will give *it* you. Hitherto have ye asked nothing in my name: ask, and ye shall receive, that your joy may be full." To pray in the name of Jesus is not to literally use those words, as in ending the prayer, "in Jesus' name, amen." Those words are fine to use, but the point of praying in Jesus' name is to pray in faith in the person, works, and authority of the Son, who made such prayer possible when he died on the cross as a propitiation for our sins and instructed his disciples to pray "in my name" in anticipation of his continuing high priestly role. Here in First John, it is the Christian's continuing belief "on the name of the Son of God" that provides a **confidence** that when we **ask any thing according to his will, he heareth us.** John is characteristically ambiguous with his pronouns, no doubt because our request is either **according to** the Father's and the Son's **will**, or contrary to both.

John continued, **if we know that he hear us, whatsoever we ask, we know that we have the petitions that we desired of him**. This is obviously not a promise that sufficient faith that God will give us what we want will result in God giving us what we want. Often, the most unloving thing to do is give someone what they want. This matter of praying **according to his will** is not a matter of saying the words. "Lord, if it be your will, please...." Rather, such prayer flows naturally for those that walk in intimate fellowship with God and enjoy the mutually abiding relationship of "us in God" and "God in us." According to what we have already read earlier in the epistle, this happens as we live out the new nature within us (God's seed) by the power of the Holy Spirit and experience the love of God perfected in us. It is unsurprising that from such a walk with the Lord we would pray **according to his will**. John's readers were no longer praying from mere human desires but from a perspective that reflected the character of God with whom they were enjoying a mutual sharing as they continued in fellowship. Given the centrality of God-love for the brethren, our prayer life should reflect such God-love for others. This person can **know that he hear** us and therefore in **confidence** also **know that we have the petitions that we desired of him**. I would submit that it is when we fall out of fellowship that we are prone to praying our own will. We do well to meditate on what this confident prayer life looks like in nuts and bolts terms. What types of things is this person praying for and not praying for? If you are not certain, I encourage you to start with reading the apostle Paul's prayers peppered throughout his epistles and see how they align with your own.

> **1 John 5:16** If any man see his brother sin a
> sin *which is* not unto death, he shall ask,

and he shall give him life for them that sin
not unto death. There is a sin unto death: I
do not say that he shall pray for it. 17 All
unrighteousness is sin: and there is a sin not
unto death.

Continuing on the issue of praying according to God's will
in confidence that such prayers will be answered, John
briefly addressed the matter of praying for fellow Christians
who are engaging in **sin**. On the one hand, a Christian
brother may **sin a sin which is not unto death**, in which case
we should **ask** or pray for him and God **shall give him life
for them that sin not unto death**. On the other hand, **there
is a sin unto death** and Christians are not instructed to **pray
for it**. In this passage, John clearly had in mind literal **death**
for which there could be no reprieve during this lifetime. It
is possible for Christians to engage in behavior that results
in divine discipline in the form of death. We see examples
of a **sin unto death** with those in Corinth who abused the
Lord's Supper (1 Corinthians 11:28-32) and with Ananias and
Sapphira who lied about their donation (Acts 5:1-11).
Practically speaking, we cannot always know when a
particular **sin** is a **sin unto death** and John did not prohibit
prayer for anyone.

John guarded against the notion that all **sin** leads to death.
He affirmed that while **all unrighteousness is sin...there is
a sin not unto death**. When the **brother** has not
committed a **sin unto death**, we can pray with confidence
that God will provide restoration to fellowship and an
experience of **life**. Based on what John wrote in 1:9, the
assumption is that restoration will follow confession, but
our prayer may result in the **brother** turning from sin and
confessing. It may also be that answered prayer that
results in a fellow Christian turning from a continuing sin

may extend that person's **life**. For example, a person who turns from alcoholism or a drug addiction to a clean and sober **life** may enjoy a longer **life**.

> **1 John 5:18** We know that whosoever is born of God sinneth not; but he that is begotten of God keepeth himself, and that wicked one toucheth him not. **19** *And* we know that we are of God, and the whole world lieth in wickedness. **20** And we know that the Son of God is come, and hath given us an understanding, that we may know him that is true, and we are in him that is true, *even* in his Son Jesus Christ. This is the true God, and eternal life.

John's final thoughts for his readers returned them to what **we** – meaning John, the apostles, and his readers – **know**. First, **whosoever is born of God sinneth not**. Though the verb **born** reads like a present tense here, the Greek reflects the perfect tense indicating a past event with continuing consequences. This is exactly what John wrote in 3:9 and means the same thing here. Namely, believers do not sin when they live out the new nature they possess by virtue of the fact that God's "seed remaineth in him." (1 John 3:9) John added that **he that is begotten** or born **of God keepeth** or guards **himself, and that wicked one toucheth him not**. Again, it is living out the new nature we have because of God's seed in us that enables us to guard against or resist sin and evil. That new nature resulting from God's seed in us is impervious to the devil and his deceptions. Of course, when we start living out the old nature or, as Paul would call it, our flesh, we can easily fall prey to Satan's attacks. (2 Corinthians 2:11; 1 Peter 5:8)

Second, John, the apostles, and his readers **know that we are of God, and the whole world lieth in wickedness.** The word **wickedness** is the Greek adjective πονηρός (poneros), which means wicked or evil, and appears here in the singular. The implied noun is "one," with the idea that the **whole word lieth** in the sway or influence of the wicked / evil one. Two entirely separate spheres are contrasted, one associated with **God** and the other in the grasp and control of Satan. It cannot be overstated how important it is that Christians be cognizant of this truth. While we need not look for deception at every turn, we do need to understand that the **world** system under Satan's control is saturated with deceptions and diversions to keep people from the truth. As Paul wrote: "In whom the god of this world hath blinded the minds of them which believe not, lest the light of the glorious gospel of Christ, who is the image of God, should shine unto them." (2 Corinthians 4:4)

Third and climactically for the entire epistle, **we know that the Son of God is come, and hath given us an understanding, that we may know him that is true.** These words brought the epistle full circle. John opened with the incarnation (1:1-3) of the "Word of Life" that the deceivers rejected. It is fitting that John closed the epistle with that same reality, grounded in historic fact, **that the Son of God is come.** Recall the foundational theological axiom John received from Jesus and shared with his readers at the beginning of his epistle, namely that "God is light, and in him is no darkness at all." On that axiom John built out his theology concerning fellowship with the Father and the Son and the mutual abiding relationship of us in God and God in us. John summarized and reiterated in closing that **the Son...hath given us an understanding** or comprehension that enables us to **know him that is true**. The **us** is inclusive of John and the apostles and John's readers. Here, John used the perfect tense of the Greek verb οἶδα (oida) for **know**. As I noted regarding John's use of oida in 3:14, this is not the verb ginoskō that John frequently used (e.g., 2:3-5) but also has a range of meaning from having information to "be[ing] intimately acquainted with or stand in a close relation to, *know*."[141] By it, John did not address how one became a child of God, but rather the Christian's experiential knowledge of **him that is true** or the **true** one. The **true** one is the **Son of God**, who is to be contrasted with the evil or wicked one of 5:19, the devil, who influences and controls the **world**. John and his readers **are of God** and enjoyed an experiential knowledge of the **Son of God**.

This level of intimacy or knowing reflected the truth-reality that they were **in** God's **Son Jesus Christ**, who **is the true God, and eternal life**. The deceivers were no doubt skilled in dressing up their lies and putting the proverbial lipstick on the pig. Many Christians have experienced having someone knock on their door offering them secret truths that pretend to ride the coattails of Christianity. Some have been offered a different Bible translation that alters the Text in numerous places to attempt to make the **Son of God** something less than and other than **the true God** John affirmed him to be. Others knock on our doors and invite us to pray about whether additional scriptures may have been written after the book of Revelation, which presupposes the way to determine canonical books is through prayer and that this is an individual enterprise. Like John's deceivers, these folks, however sincere, give

---

[141] William Arndt et al., *A Greek-English Lexicon of the New Testament*, 693.

voice to the world's lies as they cordially invite us to pray about whether there are additional scriptures. If we would but swallow that pill, they argue, we will find enlightened truth, but what they call truth denies that the **Son of God is the true God.** We must test the spirits and not fall easy prey to the lies. The battle is real and the ignorant, naïve, and gullible are at a high risk. When we **know him that is true** with the intimate knowledge that accompanies fellowship, we dwell in God's **Son Jesus Christ** and experience **the true God, and eternal life** to the fullest. From that vantage point, no matter who from the **world** knocks on the door of our minds offering counterfeits that claim superiority to experiencing **the true God, and eternal life**, we will discern their deception and continue in the truth-reality declared by **the Son of God.**

> **1 John 5:21** Little children, keep yourselves from idols. Amen.

John's final words have perplexed many because he did not previously reference the issue of **idols.** This has led some to consider John's closing words as a postscript, but his closing exhortation is no mere postscript. The word **idols** is the Greek noun εἴδωλον (eidolon) and can refer to a "cultic image/representation of an alleged transcendent being, *image, representation*"[142] or "through metonymy the image and the deity or divinity alleged to be represented"[143] by the physical representation. Here, both arguably fit the context, though the latter is probably the primary focus. Many of the religions of John's day involved physical idols and certainly he may have thought to warn his readers against such things. But more than that is in view. In this

---

[142] Ibid., 280.
[143] Ibid., 281.

final subunit (5:18-21) and closing to the epistle, John emphasized the incarnation of the Son of God, the reality that the children of God while living out their new nature do not sin and are impervious to the attacks of the devil, and that the Son of God provided us a comprehension to enjoy intimate knowledge of and fellowship with "him that is true" and "the true God, and eternal life." The deceivers of John's day and those that would come later always offer a different Jesus that is a product of the world system rather the Son of God and the true God who provides eternal life. We should not be surprised that those deceivers John labeled antichrists actually taught a distorted view of Jesus and still labeled him Jesus. Many groups today purport to speak God's Word but deny Jesus. We should expect Satan to transform himself into an angel of light and speak through those who claim to bring God's true word. All of these distortions are **idols** and the worship of them is foul and useless.

I have heard many good sermons about how Christians can make **idols** of almost anything, which is undoubtedly true, but there is something even more troubling than that. American Christianity has developed many fake Jesus **idols**. The problem with the fake Jesus is that he usually provides fake good news and falls far short of being the Son of God, the true God, and eternal life that the real Jesus is presented as in the Bible. A fake Jesus is no different than any other idol; invariably we fashion our fake Jesus to our likeness and our fake Jesus has none of those unhappy or unpleasant elements that the Biblical Jesus has. The American church wants a built-to-suit Jesus that didn't die on a cross, didn't turn over the tables of the money changers, didn't claim to be the exclusive way to the Father, and never claimed to be God with the full authority that comes with that reality.

Some of the **idols** we have made in our Jesus factory include: (1) cheerleader Jesus who only wants us to be happy and cheers us on when we do whatever we believe will make us happy; (2) good teacher Jesus who never claimed to be God or to be anything more than a man, but was a wise person who offered helpful pointers for self-improvement like loving everyone and never judging anyone for their sins; (3) gimme Jesus who dispenses good health and riches to those with enough faith that he will give them good health and riches; (4) life coach Jesus who is my always upbeat Jesus that lives for nothing more than helping me with my sense of well-being and stress management and helps me unclutter my life; (5) non-masculine Jesus, the only Jesus for the modern feminist because he never turns over the tables of the money changers or watches the super bowl because all of those toxic masculine traits have been purged; (6) pluralist Jesus who is tolerant of all beliefs no matter how much they contradict the Bible and uses an elephant illustration to show that all religious beliefs are equally valid perspectives on the same God and, indeed, Jesus is one of numerous ways to God but not the exclusive way; (7) legalist Jesus who is all about giving new arbitrary rules that ought to be in the Bible somewhere; (8) new age Jesus who is a spiritualized life force we find within ourselves through meditation and burning incense; (9) go USA Jesus who, no matter what your political platform is, that's what go USA Jesus teaches, but he never provides an honest assessment of your favorite candidate and does not expect such integrity from you; and (10) social justice Jesus who "gets us" and turned water into Marxist kool-aid but has nothing to say about sin or hell. John was spot on when he closed his epistle with the exhortation to **keep** or guard ourselves **from idols** like the fake Jesus the antichrists presented and those of our own making.

Closing

Every sermon should leave the hearers with a decision to make because God's Word is never neutral. God's Word always demands a response. First John demands a response of us. It demands a response to the truth-reality of the incarnation of the Son of God who came by the water and by the blood. It demands a response about adherence to sound apostolic doctrine. It demands a response about living in fellowship with a God who is light and in whom is no darkness at all. It calls us to a life of confession of known sins as they occur with the realization that we cannot possibly enjoy fellowship with God any other way. It calls us to a life of righteousness and love as we live out our new nature instead of the old nature. It calls us to live in a way that will produce confidence now and at the bema judgment. It demands that we know the Bible well enough to discern truth from error, and that we exercise that discernment and reject error. It implores us to let the truth of God's Word abide in us as the operative principles of our lives even in the midst of a world system that is increasingly hostile to the truth.

Application Points

- MAIN PRINCIPLE: We are overcomers if we believe that Jesus is the Son of God, who came by the water and the blood, knowing that if we have the Son we have life, and if we don't have the Son we don't have life.

- We have confidence as overcomers that if we pray according to God's will, He will grant the request except for prayers for a believer in a sin that is unto death.

- We know that as long as we live out our new nature we do not sin and cannot be touched by the devil.

- Stay away from idols including distortions of Jesus as he is presented in the Bible.

Discussion Questions

1. Why is it impossible to love God and hate a fellow believer at the same time?

2. What would it mean for a commandment to be burdensome? Why are God's commandments for us not burdensome?

3. What are the reasons for the incarnation of the Son of God? (John did not identify all of them but other texts, like Hebrews 2, provide additional reasons.)

4. If we can have confidence in prayer as John taught, what are we to conclude if our prayers are not immediately answered?

5. What are the implications of the fact that the world system is under the influence and control of Satan? How might this affect our government, media, entertainment, literature and cultural views of issues like abortion and sexuality?

6. What are some common ways people make an idol by distorting who Jesus really is?

Chapter 13

Truth Always Matters
2 John

Second and Third John are among the shortest books in the Bible, and for that reason often do not get the attention they rightly deserve. If all the scriptures are inspired – and the Bible certainly makes that claim (2 Timothy 3:16) – then we may safely infer that Second and Third John contain unique content the Holy Spirit intended for our benefit. Students of the development of the New Testament cannon with its 27 books know that First John found fairly early acceptance because it is hard to deny that its author was the same as the Fourth Gospel, which was widely accepted to be the apostle John. Second and Third John, however, were not as quickly accepted, likely owing to their brevity. After a careful study of First John, that the other two epistles issued from the same author is hardly debatable, even though the author only identifies himself as "the elder." I suggested in chapter 1 that First John was likely written between the 60s and 90s in the first century, but that the evidence was insufficient to be more precise with any confidence.

We might infer from the subject matter of all three epistles that the shorter epistles were written in or about the same general time period as First John, though we cannot say definitively in what order the three epistles were written. From the perspective of exegeting the shorter epistles, a study of First John is a tremendous aid because in the longer epistle John more fully developed some of the concepts only briefly mentioned in his shorter letters.

Just as First John is a prescient writing for modern American churches, so also is Second John. In this short epistle, John characterized what a healthy local church looks like, warned against the potential losses believers will experience at the bema judgment and in their daily walks if they are led astray by doctrine that undermines the truth of the incarnation, and sternly exhorted his readers to provide no support for those who advance teachings that undermine the incarnation. Second John is a wake-up call to local churches that downplay the importance of doctrine, to Christians who believe that sound doctrine is not that important in their lives now and in the world to come so long as they just "love Jesus," and to America's pluralistic tendencies that are all too willing to pay the intellectual costs of living with beliefs riddled with contradictions to avoid saying that anyone is wrong. Second John reminds us that truth always matters.

Outline

I.   Prologue: The Distinguished Church (1-3)

    a. John wrote to a local church he loved in accordance with the truth (1)

    b. This truth abided in John and his readers and would ultimately do so forever (2)

    c. John desired blessings for the local church grounded in truth and love (3)

II. The Distinguished Church's Members Walk in Truth (4-11)

    a. Stay On the Path of Truth (4-6)

        i. John rejoiced that he met members of the church walking in truth (4)

        ii. John exhorted the church members to love one another, as they had learned from the beginning of their Christian walks (5-6)

    b. Don't Be Led Astray By Antichrists / Deceivers (7-11)

        i. There are many antichrists / deceivers that reject the incarnation (7)

        ii. Keep up your guard so that you do not lose out on a full reward at the bema and lose fellowship with the Father and the Son (8-9)

        iii. Don't support the antichrists / deceivers in any way (10)

        iv. Supporting the antichrists / deceivers in any way is participating in their sin (11)

III. John Looked Forward to Meeting in Person (12-13)

    a. John had more to say but that would wait until he could visit the church (12)

    b. The distinguished local church John wrote from sent its greetings (13)

Scripture and Comments

This shorter epistle of John reflects certain language and ideas we saw in First John, but it is critical that the student of Second John benefit from the similarities without overlooking the unique content of Second John and how it adds to our overall understanding of fellowship. We would lose a wealth of treasure if this epistle had never been written.

> **2 John 1** The elder unto the elect lady and her children, whom I love in the truth; and not I only, but also all they that have known the truth; **2** For the truth's sake, which dwelleth in us, and shall be with us for ever. **3** Grace be with you, mercy, *and* peace, from God the Father, and from the Lord Jesus Christ, the Son of the Father, in truth and love.

John referenced himself simply as **the elder**, which translates the Greek noun πρεσβύτερος (presbuteros) and can simply refer to an elderly person or to the church office of an **elder**. Without any indication that John intended the term as a formal title, it is best understood as simply a reference to his age. No doubt his readers knew who he was, and likely among them he was referred to as **the elder** and that reflected affection and respect. John wrote to **the elect lady and her children**. Given the reference to **her children** and John's switch in verse 6 from the singular "you" to the plural "you" through verse 12, then back to the singular "you," there is little question John was writing to a local church, and by extension its members, personified as **the elect lady**. Neither First John nor Third John used the adjective **elect**. Unfortunately, through the influence of Reform Theology, many expositors infuse the adjective **elect** with a theological significance not inherent in the lexical meaning of the word, and contrary to the context of most of its usages. Without chasing this rabbit too far, a short excursion will be helpful. Like many Greek words, this one has a range of meanings and context must drive which meaning fits here. The predominant meaning of **elect**, by the time of John's writing, was not that something or someone was selected, but that something or someone had distinguishing or excellent qualities as compared to other like things or persons, and that is the meaning that fits here.

The Greek adjective translated **elect** is ἐκλεκτός (*eklektos*), and according to BDAG, it may mean "pertaining to being selected," but may also mean "pertaining to being especially distinguished" (referencing as an example the "elect angels" or "distinguished angels" of 1 Timothy 5: 21) and "pertaining to being considered best in the course of a selection, choice, excellent."[144] For the latter definition, BDAG cites numerous examples in the Bible and other Greek literature. It is notable that the word was frequently used in the Septuagint (the Greek translation of the Old Testament) and other literature with the predominant meaning of something or someone being choice, distinguished, or excellent in comparison to other like things or to someone's peers. To list several examples from the Septuagint where the adjective **elect** has nothing whatever to do with being selected: "choice" sepulchres (Genesis 23:6), "well favoured" animals (Genesis 41:2, 4, 18, 20), "rank" corn (Genesis 41:7), "chosen [i.e., the best] chariots" (Exodus 14:7), "pure myrrh" (Exodus 30:23),

---

144 William Arndt et al., *A Greek-English Lexicon of the New Testament*, 306.

"young men" (Numbers 11:28; 2 Kings 8:12; Isaiah 40:30; Lamentations 1:15, 5:13-14), "choice vows" (Deuteronomy 12:11), "chosen [i.e., the best] men" (Judges 20:15, 34; 1 Samuel 24:2, 26:2; Judith 2:15; 1 Maccabees 9:5, 15:26; Psalm 78:31), "pure" (2 Samuel 22:27; Psalm 18:26), "fat oxen" and "fatted fowl" (1 Kings 4:23), "choice fir trees" (2 Kings 19:23), "choice... men" (1 Chronicles 7:40), "great stones" (Ezra 5:8), "choice sheep" (Nehemiah 5:18), "best horseman" (1 Maccabees 4:1), "dainties" or food delicacies (Psalm 141:4), "choice silver" (Proverbs 8:19), tried or refined "hearts" (Proverbs 17:3), "excellent... cedars" (Song of Solomon 5:15), "choice" child (Song of Solomon 6:9), "plenteous" meat (Habakkuk 1:16), the "pleasant land" (Zechariah 7:14; Jeremiah 3:10), "choicest valleys" (Isaiah 22:7), "precious cornerstone" (Isaiah 28:16), "polished shaft" (Isaiah 49:2), "pleasant stones" (Isaiah 54:12), "valiant men" (Jeremiah 46:15), "pleasant vessel" (Jeremiah 25:34), and "precious clothes" (Ezekiel 27:20).

For an extra-biblical example contemporaneous with the New Testament writings, the writings of Philo (20 BC – AD 50) are informative on the usage of *eklektos*. In his writings, the patriarch Abraham is referred to as the "great father of sounds" in Cherubim 7 (with "great" translating *eklektos*), and the "elect father of sounds" in several places. Philo explained his usage of **elect**: "The word 'elect' belongs to the mind of the wise man, for whatever is most excellent is found in him." (Names 69) And in another place: "And by the addition of the word elect his goodness is intimated. For the evil disposition is a random and confused one, but that which is elect is good, having been selected from all others by reason of its excellence." (Abraham 83) As we see, *eklektos* is not about being selected for anything, but having excellent qualities.

Returning back to our text, John's purpose in describing the local church he wrote to as **elect** was to recognize that the church had distinguished herself with an excellent quality. We need not guess at how **the elect lady** had distinguished herself because John specifically praised her members or **children** for walking in truth (2 John 4). John followed his greeting to **the elect lady** with the words, **whom I love in the truth.** That is to say, John loved this local church and its members **in** accordance with **the truth.** As I presented in the first chapter, John typically used the word **truth,** the Greek noun ἀλήθεια (alētheia) to refer to a right view of reality anchored in God as declared by the Son during the incarnation, including the working out of God's redemptive plan through the Son and the Spirit. I previously referred to this as the truth-reality. His readers were grounded in the same truth-reality that grounded John's love. Anything less would be a worldly shadow of love at best. John added, **and not I only, but also all they that have known the truth.** Here he used the verb γινώσκω (ginōskō) in the perfect tense, indicating he referred to others who had come to a knowledge of **the truth** in the past with a continuing status of knowing. John's point was simply that all those grounded in the **truth** would also have the same **love** for **the elect lady and her children.**

Continuing his greeting, John explained the reason for this **love.** It was **for the truth's sake, which dwelleth in us, and shall be with us for ever.** This **truth** included, as John emphasized throughout First John, the reality of the incarnation of the Son of God who gave his life as a propitiation and is the savior of the world. John knew that we love God because He loved us first, and that we cannot love God without loving His children. This was why John and others **that have known the truth** loved this church and **her children.** Not only that, but **the truth** dwelled **in us.** This is the familiar verb μένω (menō) that is variously translated in John's writings as dwell, remain, or abide. The truth-reality of God's love expressed through the Son's incarnation and death on a cross compelled their love for one another, and this truth-reality remained **in us,** meaning John and his readers and others as an operative guiding influence in their daily walk. We know from First John that this was a hallmark of fellowship with **the Father** and **the Son.**

John's words, **and shall be with us for ever,** have been understood by some to mean that **the truth** will persist among Christians **for ever** through evangelism and discipleship. This does not seem to be the best fit, however, because John related **the truth** abiding **in us** and **shall be with us for ever.** The phrase **shall be** is the future tense of the verb εἰμί (eimi), which means to be. John thus confirmed that this abiding **truth** would in the future be a permanent part of who they are. This makes perfect sense given John's statement in First John that "when he shall appear, we shall be like him; for we shall see him as he is." (1 John 3:2) Jesus claimed to be **the truth,** and if we are to be like him, then **the truth...shall be with us for ever.**

John capped off his opening greeting with a blessing: **grace be with you, mercy, and peace, from God the Father, and from the Lord Jesus Christ, the Son of the Father, in truth and love.** John not only desired that his readers enjoy **grace, mercy, and peace,** but that they understand from whom these blessings flow, namely **God the Father** as well as **Jesus,** who is **Lord** and **Christ** or Messiah and **the Son of the Father.** The deceivers addressed in First John were also in the background of

Second John and they denied the incarnation of the **Son of** God. In both epistles, John emphasized this reality from the beginning. To say that **Jesus** is **Lord** is an express affirmation of his authority and deity. He is also the **Christ** or Messiah who died for the sins of the world. He is also **the Son of the Father**, who perfectly declared **the Father** through the incarnation. These blessings were theirs **in truth and love**, that is, grounded in the reality of **the Father** and **the Son** who in their persons are **truth and love**. In a world of counterfeits, the blessings were authentic and pure and sourced in God's **love**.

> **2 John 4** I rejoiced greatly that I found of thy children walking in truth, as we have received a commandment from the Father. **5** And now I beseech thee, lady, not as though I wrote a new commandment unto thee, but that which we had from the beginning, that we love one another. **6** And this is love, that we walk after his commandments. This is the commandment, That, as ye have heard from the beginning, ye should walk in it.

Second John is a book of commendation to a healthy local church as evidenced by the lives of its members. John **rejoiced greatly** when he **found of thy children walking in truth, as we have received a commandment from the Father**. John had become personally acquainted with some of the church members and they were living their lives in accordance with **the truth**. As we have seen, John's usage of **truth** refers to God's reality, but John's words **as we have received a commandment from the Father** pointed to a specific command that was obeyed by these church members. The verses that follow confirm that it is the command **that we love one another**. Only here did John explicitly attribute this **commandment** to **the Father**, but he also explained that **this is the commandment, that, as ye have heard from the beginning, ye should walk in it.** (compare 1 John 3:11) From **the beginning** of their Christian experience, they had been taught this central command. John similarly recorded in First John: "And this is his commandment, That we should believe on the name of his Son Jesus Christ, and love one another, as he gave us commandment." (1 John 3:23) Moreover, John recorded Jesus' words in the Fourth Gospel: "For I have not spoken of myself; but the Father which sent me, he gave me a commandment, what I should say, and what I should speak." (John 12:49) So we are to understand that the command to **love one another** came from **the Father** through the Son, and then was repeated by John and the other apostles. The believers John had met lived out the command to **love one another** and so walked **in truth**.

In view of their exemplary testimony, John wrote, **now I beseech** or implore **thee, lady...that we love one another**. Just as John had become personally acquainted with some of her **children** who exhibited **love** for **one another**, John implored the entire congregation (**lady**) to do the same. This does not mean they were not already doing so. John was merely exhorting that everyone in the church follow the example of those he'd met already. John added, **and this is love, that we walk after his commandments**. We **love** God through obedience, especially by keeping the command to **love one another**. In fact, he explained in First John that it was not possible to **love** God and not **love** His children. (1 John 4:20-5:1) John's readers received this command **from the beginning** of their Christian experience and **should walk** or live **in it**. Above all, **love** should characterize who they are just as John proclaimed that "God is love." (1 John 4:8, 16) As John explained in his longest epistle, keeping this command is the difference between abiding in life or death (1 John 3:14), knowing that "we are of the truth" or not (1 John 3:19), and enjoying mutual abiding with God or not (1 John 3:24).

> **2 John 7** For many deceivers are entered into the world, who confess not that Jesus Christ is come in the flesh. This is a deceiver and an antichrist.

As with First John, this shorter epistle provided confirmation and encouragement to his readers before offering caution concerning the **many deceivers** that have **entered into the world** system. In First John, he wrote: "Little children, it is the last time: and as ye have heard that antichrist shall come, even now are there many antichrists; whereby we know that it is the last time." (1 John 2:18) John first called out the false teachers in terms of their actions (**deceivers**) then of their purpose (**antichrist**). The word **deceivers** translates the Greek adjective πλάνος (planos) that here functions like a noun to refer to people who seek to lead astray through deceit. John stated the content of their deceit in the negative – they **confess not that Jesus Christ is come in the flesh**. Their denial of the incarnation was exactly what the **antichrists** in the crosshairs of First John were guilty of, and no doubt John had the same group in mind. Switching to the singular, John concluded, **This is a deceiver and an antichrist**, or in other words, **This** *person* **is the deceiver and the antichrist**. The word **antichrist** is the Greek ἀντίχριστος (antikristos) meaning an adversary or enemy of the Messiah. We know from First John 2:18 that, in John's thinking, there is a coming **antichrist** and in his present time (and ours) "are there many antichrists; whereby we know that it is the last time." (1 John 2:18) The person that will be *the* **antichrist** is the subject of many passages outside of John's writings such as Daniel 7:8-9 (the "little horn"), 2 Thessalonians 2:1-12 (the "son of perdition"), and Revelation 13 (the "beast...out of the sea"). John's point here is that each of the false teachers is **a deceiver and an antichrist** proleptic of the ultimate **deceiver / antichrist** to come.

> **2 John 8** Look to yourselves, that we lose not those things which we have wrought, but that we receive a full reward.

In light of the deceivers / antichrists out to convince John's readers the incarnation never happened, John warned them to **look to yourselves**, or in other words, to be on the lookout for them. John's concern was **that we lose not those things which we have wrought** or worked for, but instead that **we receive a full reward**. That John wrote here of not losing what **we** worked for tells us he was not talking about justification (salvation from sin's penalty). Instead, the issue is the coming bema judgment where our faithfulness is at issue, for which I refer the reader to the notes on First John 2:28 and 4:17-18. The reader should be aware that some modern translations use "you" instead of **we**. For example, the NIV reads, "Watch out that you do not lose what you have worked for, but that you may be rewarded fully." The KJV rendering is best, and some modern translations follow the KJV in using **we**. As Zane Hodges explains: "However a very large majority of the manuscripts read 'we' (as in NKJV) instead of 'you,' and appear to outnumber those reading 'you' by well over two to one."[145]

The question that must be answered is why John was concerned that both he and his readers stood to lose out on a **full reward** if his readers were led astray by the deceivers. Most likely, the "elect lady" was, indirectly if not directly, the fruit of John's ministry, which is confirmed by the phrase **those things which we have wrought** or worked for. If that local church, with John's help, continued walking in truth, that would translate into a more fulsome or **full reward** for John as well as the members of the church at the bema. However, if his readers were led astray and convinced to deny the incarnation, that would bring ruin to the local church and John and his readers would suffer the loss of the more fulsome **reward** that could have been theirs.

> **2 John 9** Whosoever transgresseth, and abideth not in the doctrine of Christ, hath not God. He that abideth in the doctrine of Christ, he hath both the Father and the Son.

John next stated the immediate consequences of being led astray. Following his typical formula, he stated the negative then the positive. The negative warning is that **whosoever transgresseth, and abideth not in the doctrine of Christ, hath not God**. The word **transgresseth** is the Greek verb παραβαίνω (parabainō) and can mean to turn aside or to break or transgress. Some Greek manuscripts instead have προάγω (proagō), which means "to move ahead or in front of, *go before, lead the way, precede*."[146]

---

[145] Zane Clark Hodges, *The Epistle of John*, 260.
[146] William Arndt et al., *A Greek-English Lexicon of the New Testament*, 864.

Newer translations relying on the manuscripts with proagō say something like "anyone who does not remain in Christ's teaching, but goes beyond it does not have God." In the KJV with parabainō and some newer translations with proagō, the basic idea is still essentially the same. Those who do not abide in **the doctrine** or teachings **of Christ** but instead depart from it (or go beyond it), do not have **God**. From a "tests for life" perspective (see chapter 1), John was saying that when a person departs from Jesus' teachings, they prove they are not genuine Christians. The context, however, concerns a warning to believers, many of whom John personally knew were walking in truth, about the dangers of departing from that truth. If we insist that John was concerned about spurious Christians, then it is difficult to avoid the conclusion that their departure from walking in the truth would cause them to lose their salvation, which is an obvious error. As throughout First John, the tests for life view is unworkable.

John never questioned his reader's salvation, for otherwise his first warning in the prior verse would not have concerned losses at the bema, a warning that could only apply to believers. Instead, the warning concerned his reader's experience of **God**. The word **abideth** is the familiar verb menō used throughout First John in relation to fellowship, and means to continue or remain. The **doctrine of Christ** especially has in mind the incarnation and its implications, which of course was what the deceivers rejected. In the closing chapter of First John, he emphasized that Jesus came by the water (baptism) and the blood (cross), and that through the incarnation it was made possible for God to give us eternal life "in his Son." (1 John 5:6, 11-12) The consequence of not continuing **in** the doctrine of Christ was not having God, which presumes a status of having God prior to departing. John's warning, then, equated turning aside from the doctrine of Christ to turning aside from God in their walk. The nearest warning in First John is that a failure to love equates to the believer abiding in death (1 John 3:14), where "death" is indicative of feeling distanced from God. John addressed the same idea here, and his words make perfect sense. Doctrine matters. Some Christians foolishly downplay doctrine because they are "just interested in loving Jesus," but John's point is that believers with bad doctrine concerning the person of Jesus Christ are deceived concerning their walk with God.

On the positive side, the believer that abideth or remains or continues in the doctrine of Christ has both the Father and the Son. This positive result is continuing fellowship with the Father and the Son, which of course is not possible for those that reject sound doctrine of Christ. It is to be noted that John did not say the person that abides in sound doctrine "has God," though no doubt that is true. For John, the centrality of sound Christology needed to be emphasized because that was where the deceivers were attacking, and that remains where deceivers attack today. The crux of their lie is that you can have God without the Son of God, who became flesh and dwelt among us. The apostle wrote that a believer who continues in the sound doctrine of Christ enjoys fellowship with the Father and the Son.

> 2 John 10 If there come any unto you, and bring not this doctrine, receive him not into *your* house, neither bid him God speed:
> 11 For he that biddeth him God speed is partaker of his evil deeds.

Targeting the deceivers / antichrists, John exhorted his readers, **if there come any unto you, and bring not this doctrine, receive him not into your house, neither bid him God speed**. At the time John wrote, it was a cultural norm to show hospitality to travelers, and especially for Christians to show hospitality to fellow Christian travelers. The deceivers may have been non-believers, or believers that had been led astray by pre-Gnostic pagan influences, or a mix of the two. Either way, John's readers were not to provide hospitality by inviting the deceivers into their homes, nor even by expressing fellowship. In our modern pluralistic culture, far too many Christians are unwilling to say that anyone is wrong about the scriptures, largely because the scriptures and sound doctrine are unimportant. They would rather say the scriptures are ambiguous than accuse others of twisting them. To be sure, there are areas of reasonable disagreement among Christians, but the issue for John was the very foundation of Christianity – that the Son of God became flesh and dwelt among us, and for the joy set before him endured the cross, and rose again. If a Christian won't take a stand for that, he or she won't take a stand for anything that matters. These weak-kneed folks try to make their pluralism sound righteous by saying that the deceivers they support are sincere, that God works through imperfect people, and that we should eat the meat and spit out the bones. When it comes to those whose teachings undermine core Christian doctrines, and especially the incarnation, there is no sitting on the fence.

John's readers were not pluralistic the way many Christians today are, but John knew they would struggle because of their natural tendency to show hospitality. John's exhortation presupposed his readers would know something about the beliefs of those Christians who sought hospitality from them. There is a clear application for us today. We must vet those we support. Before we send our children off to a "Christian college," it is incumbent upon us to conduct due diligence on the school's doctrine. We must determine where a person or organization stands before we align with them, and this includes joining a new church, inviting a special guest speaker, recommending a book, adopting a curriculum for the youth department, and much more. According to John, those **that biddeth** the deceiver **God speed is partaker of his evil deeds**. Regardless of whether we knowingly embrace the deceivers, or do so ignorantly or through a failure to conduct our due diligence, when we support the deceivers in any way we partner in their **evil deeds**, assisting their ministry of deception.

> **2 John 12** Having many things to write unto you, I would not *write* with paper and ink: but I trust to come unto you, and speak face to face, that our joy may be full. **13** The children of thy elect sister greet thee. Amen.

In closing, John shared that he had **many things to write unto** the members of the local church he addressed, but he preferred **not** to **write with paper and ink**. John looked forward to visiting them in person so he could **speak face to face, that our joy may be full**. John's final remark confirmed he wrote from another local church, and he sent greetings from its members, **the children of thy elect sister**. John wrote to a church to be highly commended, and therefore referred to that local body of believers as an **elect** or distinguished "lady." He likewise commended the local church where he was at as an **elect** or distinguished **sister** or fellow local body to his readers. His final word for them, a simple **amen**. He trusted he would see them soon.

Closing

It is easy today to conclude there are no good local churches and opt not to be a part of one. I know some people live in areas where there really are none, and perhaps they should plant a local church committed to sound doctrine but of course not everyone can do that. Most Christians in America have access to a good but not perfect local church and need to be there because this was neither my idea, their idea, nor John's idea, but Jesus' idea. He proclaimed in Matthew 16 that he would build his church, and the book of Acts relates the early history of Jesus' building project, which is actualized in local churches throughout the world. That's his plan, and to say you want nothing to do with any local church anywhere is to say you want nothing to do with the primary ministry of Jesus Christ in the world at this time. That the apostles were routinely involved in planting, ministering to, and writing to local churches confirms this. Second John tells us there can be healthy local churches and the most basic ingredient is sound Christology. If John thought he were writing to a perfect church he hardly needed to waste the paper and ink. John knew he was writing to a good church composed of imperfect people doing life together. That kind of local church has something for us, and perhaps in Jesus' plans we have something for it. We need to be a part of such a church. At the same time, we need to heed John's warning and any church that is not grounded on the reality of the incarnation, that the Son of God came by the water and the blood, that he really died for the sins of the world and rose again, is no church at all and must be avoided.

Application Points

- MAIN PRINCIPLE: A local church should be distinguished by its members walking in truth, especially the truth of the incarnation of the Son of God, and the command to love one another.

- Christians must not be led astray by deceivers who undermine the incarnation because to do so will result in not receiving a full reward at the bema and not being in fellowship with the Father and the Son.

- Christians must not support churches, ministries, and teachers who do not uphold as a core tenant the incarnation of the Son of God.

Discussion Questions

1. In practical terms, what does it look like for a person to walk in truth?

2. How would an elect or distinguished local church differ from one that is not elect or distinguished?

3. How should a Christian live knowing that many deceivers are in the world?

4. In the United States, we do not generally have hospitality practices for traveling Christian teachers involving opening up individual's homes. What are some application points for modern Christians of John's exhortation to provide neither hospitality nor a greeting to deceivers?

Chapter 14

Reputation Matters

3 John

The short epistle we refer to as Third John packs a punch. It is a very personal letter that was addressed to an individual named Gaius who had a good reputation. To those Christians who would say, "I don't care what other people think about me," the apostle John, under the inspiration of the Holy Spirit, wrote that the Christian's reputation matters. A good reputation for living in accordance with the truth is commendable. A bad reputation for not living in accordance with the truth is inexcusable. Obviously, it is possible to have a bad reputation among bad people because we are doing good, but it is easy to be self-deceived in this area. It is easy to convince ourselves that our bad reputation is an attack on our beliefs when it is instead a reaction to our ungodly words and actions. Even lost people can spot a hypocrite. Third John also recognized a phenomenon anyone who has been in local churches a while has witnessed – usurpers. These people position themselves to exercise authority they don't rightly possess and they drive away any potential threats to their usurpation. Many a good pastor has resigned after discovering that usurpers dominate the church nullifying his ability to lead. Like all of the Bible, Third John has much to say to us.

Outline

I.   John's Greeting to the Well-Beloved Gaius (1)

II. The Good Reputation of Gaius (2-8)

   a. John prayed that Gaius would enjoy good health and would live for God (2)

   b. John rejoiced in the good report he received about Gaius (3-4)

   c. Gaius had a good reputation for hospitality and generosity to traveling missionaries (5-6a)

   d. Gaius would do well to continue his generosity to missionaries because their efforts were in response to Jesus' exalted status and authority (6a-7)

   e. Providing for missionaries' needs is a way to participate in their work (8)

III. The Bad Reputation of Diotrephes the Usurper (9-11)

   a. In contrast to Gaius, Diotrephes rebuffed the apostle as a rival to his usurped authority over the local church to which Gaius was a member (9)

   b. Diotrephes slandered John and others with John, and prevented others from providing for traveling missionaries (10)

c. Don't follow Diotrephes' example, which reflects a lack of fellowship with God, but instead do the right thing (11)

d. Provide for Demetrius, who has a good reputation (12)

IV. John Looks Forward to Meeting Gaius in Person (13-14)

a. John had more to say but that would wait until he could come in person (13)

b. John and his friends greet Gaius and ask that he pass along greetings to those he would consider friends to John (14)

Scripture and Comments

In one sense, this very personal epistle had a narrow purpose of securing provision for a traveling Christian named Demetrius from another Christian of good report named Gaius. In the broader sense, in its thirteen verses, Third John addressed the importance of the Christian's reputation as well as the disastrous consequences of persons in local churches who usurp and abuse the authority over a church that is only rightfully held by Jesus Christ.

3 John 1 The elder unto the wellbeloved Gaius, whom I love in the truth.

John introduced himself as **the elder**, which translates the Greek noun πρεσβύτερος (presbuteros) and here simply means an elderly person. Given John's use of the same words in Second John, we may infer that John had become known as "the **elder**." No doubt his readers knew who he was, and John's identification as **the elder** reflected affection and respect. John wrote to **the wellbeloved Gaius**. The word **wellbeloved** is the Greek adjective ἀγαπητός (agapētos) and means pertaining "to one who is dearly loved, *dear, beloved, prized, valued.*"[147] In this context, it suggests a close friendship between the apostle and **Gaius**. There are references elsewhere in the New Testament to men named Gaius (e.g., Acts 19:29, 20:4; Romans 16:23; 1 Corinthians 1:14), but there is no reason to identify John's friend with these others. Our knowledge of **Gaius** is limited to what we read in Third John, though we can infer that he was "[m]ost likely a wealthy Christian, since he is noted for his hospitality."[148] John added, **whom I love in the truth**, which mirrors what he wrote of "the elect lady and her children" in Second John 1.

John loved **Gaius... in** accordance with **the truth**. As I presented in the first chapter of this commentary, John typically used the word **truth**, the Greek noun ἀλήθεια (alētheia), to refer to a right view reality anchored in God as declared by the Son during the incarnation, including the working out of God's redemptive plan through the Son and the Spirit. I previously referred to this as the truth-reality. John understood that genuine **love** cannot be divorced from **the truth** because **love** is an attribute of God, and the person of God is the cornerstone of the truth-reality. This is important for modern Christians in a culture where the word **love** is overused and misapplied. John loved **Gaius** with the quality of **love** that God is.

> **3 John 2** Beloved, I wish above all things that thou mayest prosper and be in health, even as thy soul prospereth.

---

[147] William Arndt et al., *A Greek-English Lexicon of the New Testament*, 7.

[148] John D. Barry et al., eds., "Gaius, Addressee of 3 John," *The Lexham Bible Dictionary* (Bellingham, WA: Lexham Press, 2016).

Here, John repeated the adjective ἀγαπητός (agapetos) that was translated "wellbeloved" in Third John 1. Again, it indicates a close relationship or friendship between John and Gaius. John wrote, **I wish above all things.** The word **wish** is the Greek verb εὔχομαι (euchomai) that has a primary meaning "to pray" and secondary meaning "to wish." Given the Christian context it seems more likely that the apostle would share with Gaius that he was praying for him rather than merely wishing. In any event, John's desire was that Gaius **mayest prosper and be in** good **health, even as thy soul prospereth.** That John wished or prayed for his friend's good **health** is easy to understand, and confirms to us the rather obvious point that we should pray for the good **health** of others. The latter part of John's prayer needs more careful attention. English readers typically understand **soul** to mean the non-material part of us or the spirit, which in this context begs the question of what it would mean for Gaius' immaterial part or spirit to prosper. Almost certainly, the word does not have that meaning here, and a short excursus on this word will be beneficial.

The word **soul** is the Greek noun ψυχή (psyche) and has different meanings in different contexts, but is not the same as the word "spirit" (pneuma). David Anderson explains that there are four New Testament uses of "soul" but that the term only rarely refers to the immaterial aspect of man that can go to heaven or hell:

> The word *psyche* is used in four primary ways in the NT. Only a handful of the 104 uses refer to the immaterial part of man, which enjoys heaven or suffers in hell. Most of the time, the word refers either to our

time on earth (our life) or to our inner self as a unique combination of mind (with one *psyche* striving together—Phil. 2:17), emotions (Mk 14:34—my *psyche* is exceedingly sorrowful), and will (doing the will of God from the *psyche*).[149]

We frequently see *psyche* translated as "soul" or "life" in our New Testaments. One use of **soul** is for the principle of life or being alive, as in Acts 20:10 (Eutychus fell out of the window and apparently died but "Paul went down, and fell on him, and embracing him said, Trouble not yourselves; for his **life** is in him."). Another use is for a living human being, as in 1 Corinthians 15:44 ("The first man Adam was made a living soul...."). Yet another use is to refer to the entire immaterial aspect of man, as in Matthew 10:28 ("And fear not them which kill the body, but are not able to kill the **soul**: but rather fear him which is able to destroy both **soul** and body in hell."). And the fourth use is the experience of life, which may refer to experiences within the inner self as Anderson notes, or to the entire experience. Harry Leafe explains that in the context of verses like James 1:21, *psyche* "describes the whole of a person's life" and "can be defined as *the total temporal expression of human life*."[150] For verses where the experience of life is at issue, we might express the meaning as the "soul-life."

John prayed that Gaius, in addition to good physical **health** would also enjoy a healthy or prospering soul-life. Sometimes we think about how someone has lived,

---

[149] David R. Anderson, *Triumph through Trials: The Epistle of James* (Grace Theology Press, 2013), 33.

[150] G. Harry Leafe, *Running to Win!*, 4-5.

especially when we think of an older person we respect or perhaps as we remember someone's life after they have died. We might say that this person lived well or that his or her life was a testimony to certain virtues or we might remember some of their accomplishments. We might also follow this line of thought for someone whose life we believe was largely squandered. These reflections concern the person's soul-life. John prayed for Gaius that he would, from a uniquely Christian perspective, live out his soul-life well.

> **3 John 3** For I rejoiced greatly, when the brethren came and testified of the truth that is in thee, even as thou walkest in the truth. **4** I have no greater joy than to hear that my children walk in truth.

We should understand from the Bible that works play no role in our justification, but we should also understand that the expectation of Jesus and the apostles was that over time Christians would mature and be transformed. (e.g., Romans 12:1-2) From John's perspective, a central component of the maturing process was walking in fellowship with the Father and the Son. Many Christians today are rightly concerned that maturity and transformation might seem more the exception than the rule, largely because of a lack of Biblical literacy. Based on John's witness, Gaius was the proverbial real McCoy, and his transformed life was a visible testimony to those around him. John **rejoiced greatly when the brethren came and testified of the truth that is in thee, even as thou walkest in the truth**. What John confirmed, and rejoiced in, was that Gaius had a good reputation because he had **the truth...in** him as a guiding principle for living, and because he lived out **the truth** in words and actions. As before, we are to understand **the truth** broadly as God's reality that was declared by the Son during his incarnation. It includes his express teachings like loving one another as well as his exhibiting the character of God. When a Christian walks **in truth** he or she makes God's character, including His love, visible.

Gaius' reputation pleased John, who found **no greater joy than to hear that** his **children walk in truth**. This, of course, should be the goal of every teacher or preacher of God's Word, and of everyone involved in disciple-making. It is not good enough that people would learn **the truth**, but that **the truth** would be in them as the guiding principle so that it bears out in their daily **walk**. Seeing lives transformed by **the truth** should be the greatest joy to those who minister to others, as it was for John who had ministered to Gaius.

> **3 John 5** Beloved, thou doest faithfully whatsoever thou doest to the brethren, and to strangers; **6** Which have borne witness of thy charity before the church: whom if thou bring forward on their journey after a godly sort, thou shalt do well: **7** Because that for his name's sake they went forth, taking nothing of the Gentiles.

Again using the adjective ἀγαπητός (agapētos) that he used in Third John 1 and 2, John referred to Gaius as **beloved** or dear friend. Gaius had a reputation for doing **faithfully whatsoever** he did for **the brethren**, meaning fellow Christians, and for **strangers**. While in isolation one might conclude that **strangers** means non-Christians, verse 6 renders that option highly improbable because both groups, **the brethren** and the **strangers**, bore **witness of** Gaius' **charity before the church**. Also, most manuscripts include the article "the" before **strangers**, suggesting an identified group. Given the heavy focus in the balance of the epistle on hospitality, Gaius' reputation was for providing for the needs of **the brethren**, meaning traveling Christians he knew, as well as the **strangers**, meaning traveling Christians he did not personally know. In both cases, it was travelling missionaries Gaius assisted in their journeys. John affirmed, **because that for his name's sake they went forth, taking nothing of the Gentiles**, meaning from the non-Christians. These travelers did not look to non-believers for financial support, but instead looked to find support from God's people.

The word **charity** is the familiar ἀγάπη (agapē), often translated love, and means volitional love that does for others. Gaius provided for travelling missionaries, and his **charity** or love was observed by others who bore **witness of** his **charity before the** local **church** where John was located, which prompted John to write the epistle. John confirmed to Gaius that he would **do well** by sending the missionaries **forward on their journey after a godly sort**, that is, in a manner worthy of God. In other words, John expected from Gaius' reputation that he would send the missionaries **forward on their journey** well-supplied and cared for precisely because their journey was **for his name's sake**, or for the **sake** of the **Name**. We are best to understand that these missionaries were carrying out the Great Commission (e.g., Matthew 28:18-20). They should be provided for generously for the sake of the **Name** of Jesus Christ, the Son of God. Remember that the **Name** is not the word "Jesus" but a reference to his exalted status and reputation as the one with all authority.

(e.g., Matthew 28:18; Hebrews 1:2) As Paul commented, "Wherefore God also hath highly exalted him, and given him a name which is above every name." (Philippians 2:9) Gaius' provision for the missionaries should be appropriate in view of who sent them. As Hodges states: "In other words, **God** is to be in no way disgraced by meager, half-hearted, or grudging hospitality to those who serve Him. In John's day, the need for such hospitality was magnified by the poor quality of the inns in the Roman Empire, as well as by the hostility that Christian evangelists might expect to encounter in their travels."[151]

> **3 John 8** We therefore ought to receive such, that we might be fellowhelpers to the truth.

John's application for Gaius and for us is that **we therefore ought to receive** or welcome **such, that we might be fellowhelpers to the truth**. The word **fellowhelpers** is συνεργός (synergos) and means "pert[aining] to working together with, *helping,* as subst[antive] and always so in our lit[erature] *helper, fellow-worker.*"[152] When Christians support missionaries, they are participating in the missionary endeavor. The apostle Paul made a similar statement when he thanked the Philippians for their "fellowship in the gospel from the first day until now," in reference to their provision for the apostle's needs on his missionary journey. The Great Commission still stands as our overarching directive as Christians, and one way this is carried out is by providing for those who take the gospel to the ends of the earth. Based on Gaius' reputation, he unquestionably did **receive** missionaries and provided for their needs on their journey, and therefore was a

---

151 Zane Clark Hodges, *The Epistle of John,* 282.
152 William Arndt et al., *A Greek-English Lexicon of the New Testament,* 969.

participant in their evangelistic work taking **the truth** to the world. The reason John concluded that **we** need to be diligent in this ministry was because some were not generous like Gaius, which issue John next addressed.

> **3 John 9** I wrote unto the church: but Diotrephes, who loveth to have the preeminence among them, receiveth us not. **10** Wherefore, if I come, I will remember his deeds which he doeth, prating against us with malicious words: and not content therewith, neither doth he himself receive the brethren, and forbiddeth them that would, and casteth *them* out of the church.

Having commended Gaius for his generosity to travelling missionaries, John turned to a more difficult subject, and a church member that was much the opposite of Gaius. John had written a letter **unto the** local **church** where Gaius fellowshipped. This is a good reminder that our New Testament does not contain all the letters the apostles wrote. We know, for example, that Paul wrote letters to Corinth that we don't have copies of. Likewise, John wrote a letter to the local **church** Gaius attended that has not been preserved. In any event, a **church** member named **Diotrepehes, who loveth to have the preeminence among them, receive us not**. This **Diotrephes** wanted to exercise complete authority **among them**, a reference to either the entire local **church** or possibly to the other elders at that church. Either way, he was a usurper of absolute authority over the local **church**, which is uniquely the role of Jesus Christ as the head of the body. (Ephesians 5:23; Colossians 1:18) He would not **receive** the apostle John and others, who possibly were other apostles. John's point was that he **wrote...the church** about his plans to journey to there, but **Diotrephes** refused to extend a welcome and hospitality. It is unclear whether **Diotrephes** responded to John's letter, but John learned, probably from the same group that bore witness to Gaius' support for traveling missionaries, that **Diotrephes** had no intent to welcome John. This usurpation is why John wrote to Gaius directly.

It bears pointing out that John provided no statement about whether **Diotrephes** knew "the truth," but it is clear that he did not walk in it. If John could make the journey, he would **remember** Diotrephes' **deeds which he doeth, prating against us with malicious words: and not content therewith, neither doth he himself receive the brethren, and forbiddeth them that would, and casteth them out of the church.** This man's relentless ambition and defensive measures against any potential rivals led him not only to refuse the apostle John, but to slander him and those with him (again, possibly some of the other apostles). As he was **not content** with his verbal attacks on John, **Diotrephes** refused to **receive the brethren**, meaning the traveling missionaries. Even worse, he forbade **them that would, and casteth them out of the church**. In other words, **Diotrephes** saw people like Gaius as rivals to his authority that had to be excluded from fellowship with **the church** for the "crime" of providing for traveling missionaries. Here we have a believer opposing the Great Commission.

Unfortunately, this happens more often than we'd like to admit. There are those whose personal agendas drive them to oppose the work of **the church**. I was once invited by a Baptist pastor to lead a Bible study on Sunday evenings. During my affiliation with the church the pastor proposed an aggressive evangelism effort focused on the surrounding community, whose demographic no longer matched that of most of the church members, and for this he was fired. Anytime this happens those loyal to their **Diotrephes** concoct a narrative for why the pastor had to be let go, but I distinctly recall a deacon's wife during a business meeting saying, "we don't want those people in our church." I can only imagine the letter John might have written to address what I witnessed there. In John's day, he was prepared, if he came to that church, to **remember his deeds**, meaning that in some way he would confront **Diotrephes** and hold him accountable.

> **3 John 11** Beloved, follow not that which is evil, but that which is good. He that doeth good is of God: but he that doeth evil hath not seen God.

With Diotrephes' reprehensible conduct in mind, John exhorted Gaius, his **beloved** or dear friend: **follow not** the example of **that which is evil, but that which is good.** In short, don't be like Diotrephes. John's theological commentary on the situation was that **he that doeth good is of God: but he that doeth evil hath not seen God.** In First John, he similarly wrote: "Whosoever abideth in him sinneth not: whosoever sinneth hath not seen him, neither known him." (1 John 3:6) The phrase **do good** is the Greek verb ἀγαθοποιέω (agathapoieō) and means "to do that which is beneficial to another, *do good, be benevolent, be helpful.*"[153] The verb **seen** is the Greek verb ὁράω (horaō) and can mean seeing with our eyes, but also can mean "to experience a condition or event"[154] or "to be mentally or

---

153 Ibid., 3.
154 Ibid., 719.

spiritually perceptive, *perceive.*[155] What is in view here is obviously not physical sight of God with the eyes, who John elsewhere wrote that no one has **seen** at any time (John 1:18), but instead, seeing with the comprehension and perception of one in intimate fellowship with God. John used the perfect tense, indicating a past action with continuing consequences. Those believers that do **good** are **of God**, meaning they are visibly manifested as His children in their actions, which express God's righteousness as well as love for others as they walk in fellowship. In contrast, those that do **evil** have not **seen God** in the sense of an intimate comprehension or perception linked to continued fellowship with Him. This is an important point because many Christians want to believe that Diotrephes – most of us have met him or her somewhere in some church or in the mirror – must be lost. All John concluded was that he **hath not seen God**, that is, that his conduct reflected his lack of fellowship. His flesh was in the driver seat as he pursued preeminence among people instead of fellowship with God.

John's words were not academic. John sought to obtain assistance for a man named Demetrius, whom John named in the next verse. John was aware of Gaius' reputation concerning traveling missionaries, and likewise aware that Diotrephes would provide no help and even seek to excommunicate those that would. John was counting on Gaius rejecting the example of Diotrephes and doing **good** for Demetrius.

> **3 John 12** Demetrius hath good report of all *men*, and of the truth itself: yea, and we *also* bear record; and ye know that our record is true.

---

[155] Ibid., 720.

In contrast to Diotrephes, John noted another man named **Demetrius** who, like Gaius, had a **good report** or reputation **of all men**. As I noted in the introduction, some Christians say they don't care what others think about them, but according to John a Christian should maintain a good reputation. Not only was **Demetrius** commended by others, but by **the truth itself**. His life was so aligned with **the truth** that John could say **the truth** testified on his behalf. Here was a man that "doeth good" and so was "of God." (3 John 11) Moreover, John added that **we also bear record; and ye know that our record is true**. In this way, John reached the ultimate purpose of his very personal letter to Gaius, namely that Gaius, of whom John already received good reports of his hospitality, would extend such generosity to **Demetrius** notwithstanding any opposition he might face from Diotrephes.

> **3 John 13** I had many things to write, but I will not with ink and pen write unto thee: **14** But I trust I shall shortly see thee, and we shall speak face to face. Peace *be* to thee. *Our* friends salute thee. Greet the friends by name.

In a closing similar to Second John, he expressed that he **had many** more **things to write** about, but preferred **not** to do so **with ink and pen**. Instead, John was confident that he **shall shortly see** Gaius, and at that time **we shall speak face to face**. We can only imagine the insights we might have gained if we could have listened in on that conversation. John closed with a blessing to Gaius, **peace be to thee**. Presumably in reference to those in the local church where John was located, he wrote that the **friends salute thee**, and requested that Gaius **greet the friends by**

name. John did not say **greet the** brethren. In these final words, John likely intended only that Gaius **greet the friends** in his local assembly, meaning those who would welcome such a greeting from John. This would, of course, exclude Diotrephes. As Christians, we should aspire to be **friends** with our fellow Christians, but for a variety of reasons that is not always possible. John knew that and likely intended that the contents of his letter not be shared beyond those who could rightly be considered his **friends** as others, like Diotrephes, would surely twist John's intent and use it to escalate defensive measures.

Closing

It is unfortunate that there are a lot of people like "Diotrephes" out there in the wild. They tend to flourish in churches that reject the Biblical model of leadership in a plurality of elders, but it can happen anywhere. The "Diotrophes" can be the pastor, the pastor's wife, a deacon, or just about anyone else in the local church, with the help of others who don't know or don't care about Scriptural leadership in the church. It is far easier to make a king than unmake one, and it is the unmaking of those with preeminence that usually leads to civil wars and church splits. Moreover, it may not be a single person but a group, committee, or board that seizes the authority only rightly held by Christ. Thankfully, there are also a lot of people like "Gaius" out there in the wild. These people do what they do without the need for top billing or any craving for power over others. They are in line with the Lord Jesus Christ' Great Commission and participate in it through missionary support. Gaius' reputation is memorialized in this little epistle for our benefit as an example to follow. Diotrephes' reputation is likewise memorialized for our benefit so that we would not be like him nor get behind any like him that usurp authority over the church, whether it be a particular individual or deacon board or any other group.

Application Points

- MAIN PRINCIPLE: Strive to have a good reputation based on living out the truth, including especially your treatment of others involved in Christian ministry.

- Don't usurp authority in the local church that only belongs to Jesus Christ, as the head of the body, or to his duly appointed elders.

Discussion Questions

1. Why is a good reputation important? Is it ever ok to have a bad reputation?

2. John focused on the issue of hospitality and provision for traveling Christians. What is the broader application point for us today?

3. What are the methods and motives of those like Diotrephes?

4. Does the Bible establish a structure for authority in a local church? Why is this important or not important?

5. What are ways that people may usurp authority in a church and not realize that they are usurpers like Diotrephes?

6. In a congregational church where most things are voted on, how might that usurp Jesus' authority over the local church?

Bibliography

Anderson, David R., *Maximum Joy: 1 John—Relationship or Fellowship?* Grace Theology Press, 2013.

Anderson, David R. *Triumph through Trials: The Epistle of James.* Grace Theology Press, 2013.

Arndt, William, et al. *A Greek-English Lexicon of the New Testament and Other Early Christian Literature.* Chicago: University of Chicago Press, 2000.

Barry, John D., et al., eds. "Gaius, Addressee of 3 John," *The Lexham Bible Dictionary.* Bellingham, WA: Lexham Press, 2016.

Baker, David W. "Leviticus," in *Cornerstone Biblical Commentary: Leviticus, Numbers, Deuteronomy*, ed. Philip W. Comfort, vol. 2. Carol Stream, IL: Tyndale House Publishers, 1996.

Barton, Bruce B. and Grant R. Osborne. *1, 2 & 3 John*, Life Application Bible Commentary. Wheaton, IL: Tyndale House, 1998.

Bingham, D. Jeffrey. "One God, One Christ, One Salvation," *Christian History Magazine-Issue 96: The Gnostic Hunger for Secret Knowledge.* Carol Stream, IL: Christianity Today, 2007.

Bruce, F. F. *The Epistles of John: Introduction, Exposition and Notes.* Nashville, TN; Bath, England: Kingsley Books, 2018.

Campbell, Donald K. "Foreword," in *Basic Bible Interpretation: A Practical Guide to Discovering Biblical Truth*, ed. Craig Bubeck Sr. Colorado Springs, CO: David C. Cook, 1991.

Cross, F. L. and Elizabeth A. Livingstone, eds. *The Oxford Dictionary of the Christian Church.* Oxford; New York: Oxford University Press, 2005.

Derickson, Gary W. "What Is the Message of 1 John?," *Bibliotheca Sacra* 150 (1993).

Dillow, Joseph C. *Final Destiny: The Future Reign of the Servant Kings, 4th Edition.* Houston, TX: Grace Theology Press, 2018.

Feinberg, Jeffrey Enoch, Ph.D. and Kim Alan Moudy, *Walk Leviticus!: And He Called.* Baltimore, MD: Messianic Jewish Publishers, 2001.

Harris, R. Laird. "Leviticus," in *The Expositor's Bible Commentary: Genesis, Exodus, Leviticus, Numbers*, ed. Frank E. Gaebelein, vol. 2. Grand Rapids, MI: Zondervan Publishing House, 1990.

Hodges, Zane C. "1 John," in *The Bible Knowledge Commentary: An Exposition of the Scriptures*, ed. J. F. Walvoord and R. B. Zuck, vol. 2. Wheaton, IL: Victor Books, 1985.

Hodges, Zane Clark. *The Epistle of John: Walking in the Light of God's Love.* Irving, TX: Grace Evangelical Society, 1999.

Kruse, Colin G. *The Letters of John*, The Pillar New Testament Commentary. Grand Rapids, MI; Leicester, England: W.B. Eerdmans Pub.; Apollos, 2000.

Law, Robert. *The Tests of Life*, 2d ed. Edinburgh: Clark, 1909.

Lenski, R. C. H. *The Interpretation of the Epistles of St. Peter, St. John and St. Jude.* Minneapolis, MN: Augsburg Publishing House, 1966.

Lioy, Dan. "The Biblical Concept of Truth in the Fourth Gospel," *Conspectus Volume 6* (2008).

Marshall, I. Howard. *The Epistles of John*, The New International Commentary on the New Testament. Grand Rapids, MI: Wm. B. Eerdmans Publishing Co., 1978.

McLauring, Dougald, III "Ancestry and Posterity," ed. Douglas Mangum et al., *Lexham Theological Wordbook*, Lexham Bible Reference Series. Bellingham, WA: Lexham Press, 2014.

Morris, Leon. *The Gospel according to John*, The New International Commentary on the New Testament. Grand Rapids, MI: Wm. B. Eerdmans Publishing Co., 1995.

Osborne, Grant and Philip W. Comfort. *Cornerstone Biblical Commentary, Vol 13: John and 1, 2, and 3 John.* Carol Stream, IL: Tyndale House Publishers, 2007.

Pentecost, Edward C. "Jude," in *The Bible Knowledge Commentary: An Exposition of the Scriptures*, ed. J. F. Walvoord and R. B. Zuck, vol. 2. Wheaton, IL: Victor Books, 1985.

Richards, Lawrence O. *The Teacher's Commentary.* Wheaton, IL: Victor Books, 1987.

Rooker, Mark F. *Leviticus*, vol. 3A, The New American Commentary. Nashville: Broadman & Holman Publishers, 2000.

Ross, Allen P. *Holiness to the Lord: A Guide to the Exposition of the Book of Leviticus.* Grand Rapids, MI: Baker Academic, 2002.

Sklar, Jay. *Leviticus: An Introduction and Commentary*, ed. David G. Firth, vol. 3, Tyndale Old Testament Commentaries. Nottingham, England: Inter-Varsity Press, 2013.

Sproul, R. C. *The Holiness of God*, 2nd ed. Carol Stream, IL: Tyndale House Publishers, Inc., 1998.

Thompson, Marianne Meye. *1–3 John*, The IVP New Testament Commentary Series. Downers Grove, IL: InterVarsity Press, 1992.

Tripolitis, Antonía. *Religions of the Hellenistic-Roman Age.* Grand Rapids, MI; Cambridge, U.K.: William B. Eerdmans Publishing Company, 2002.

Walvoord, John F. and Roy B. Zuck. Dallas Theological Seminary. *The Bible Knowledge Commentary: An Exposition of the Scriptures*, vol. 2. Wheaton, IL: Victor Books, 1985.

Wenham, Gordon J. *The Book of Leviticus*, The New International Commentary on the Old Testament. Grand Rapids, MI: Wm. B. Eerdmans Publishing Co., 1979.

Westcott, Brooke Foss, ed. *The Epistles of St. John: The Greek Text with Notes and Essays*, 4th ed., Classic Commentaries on the Greek New Testament. London; New York: Macmillan, 1902.

Wuest, Kenneth S. *Wuest's Word Studies from the Greek New Testament: For the English Reader*, vol. 13. Grand Rapids: Eerdmans, 1997.

About the Author

HUTSON SMELLEY resides in Chappell Hill, Texas with his wife and children. He holds advanced degrees in mathematics, law and Biblical studies, and is an adjunct professor at the College of Biblical Studies. He can be contacted at: proclaimtheword@mac.com

www.ingramcontent.com/pod-product-compliance
Lightning Source LLC
Chambersburg PA
CBHW060010050426
42448CB00012B/2683